擒拿法

SHAOLIN CHIN NA FA

The book was written by Liu Jin Sheng in collaboration with Zhao Jiang. The first edition of the book was issued in July of 1936 as a manual for the Police Academy of Zhejiang province. The book was printed by the publishing house Shan Wu in Shanghai.

Chinese Martial Arts - Theory & Practice / Old & Rare Chinese Books, Treatises, Manuscripts

shaolinkungfulibrary.com

/Old and Rare Chinese Books in English/

"If two outstanding fighters encountered in a fight, like a tiger against a tiger, the outcome of the combat depends on a measure of skill in CHIN NA..."

Shaolin Quan Shu Mi Jue (Secret Directions for Shaolin Pugilistic Art). Peking, 1915

Shaolin Kung Fu Online Library

2024

SHAOLIN CHIN NA FA

ART of SEIZING and GRAPPLING

Instructors Manual for Police Academy

of Zhejiang Province

(Shanghai, 1936)

Translated from Chinese

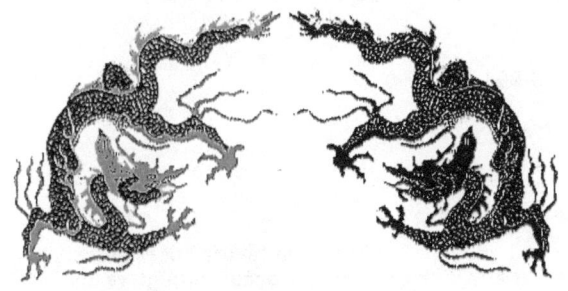

Liu Jin Sheng
Andrew Timofeevich (Translator)

*Shaolin Chin Na Fa: Art of Seizing and Grappling.
Instructor's Manual for Police Academy of Zhejiang
Province (Shanghai, 1936)*

Editor of the translation Andrew Timofeevich. Translated by Wang Ke Ze, Leonid Serbin, Ekaterina Buga, Oleg Korshunov.

Book design by Andrew Timofeevich and Olga Akimova.

Published by Shaolin Kung Fu Online Library

USA, 2024

ISBN: 979-8-9919633-5-0

shaolinkungfulibrary.com

Disclaimer:

The author and publisher of this material are not responsible in any manner whatsoever for any injury whish may occur through reading or following the instruction in this manual. The activities, physical or otherwise, described in this material may be too strenuous or dangerous for some people, and the reader should consult a physician before engaging in them.

"...If you are in command of this technique, you can sway the destiny of the enemy. You can kill your enemy, cause unbearable pain, tear his muscles and sinews, break his bones or make him unconscious for some time and completely disable him to resist.

Even a woman or a physically weak man who mastered this technique can curb a strong enemy. This technique demands deftness and skill, not brute force. It is necessary to train oneself daily to make the body flexible and nimble, but "hardness" must be hidden inside this "softness."

Liu Jin Sheng.
The Police Academy of Zhejiang Province.
1-st of May of the 24-th year of the Chinese Republic (1935)

SHAOLIN CHIN NA

"The beginnings of the Shaolin art CHIN NA trace back to many centuries. Inmost GONG FU of secret methods of CHIN NA is passed down from one generation to another to attain the highest perfection in the martial art.

When you find yourself face to face with the enemy armed with a "short" weapon, fully rely upon methods of CHIN NA and your vision. Position of the enemy, his body, his face, how he stands and what he is going to do – everything must be clearly sized up. When you understand intentions of the enemy, rely upon your own force, seize an opportunity, alternate "hard" and "soft" techniques.

If two outstanding fighters encountered in a fight, like a tiger against a tiger, the outcome of the combat depends on a measure of skill in CHIN NA. He is in the process of transforming, so do I, closely following him. Blows and grips follow continuously, without a moment's respite. You see an opening and needle your way into the vulnerable spot, clear a passage and rush forward.

If you encounter a villain, make a grip (CHIN) at first, then use the technique (FA), and you will be able to exercise a control (NA). An arm of flesh and bone can deprive even an iron man of courage. Hard to defend oneself against deft techniques, no defense against skilful finger efforts."

Shaolin Quan Shu Mi Jue (Secret Directions on
Shaolin Pugilistic Art). Peking, 1915.

Contents

Part I. TOU BU NA FA: Head Grips

Part II. JING BU NA FA: Neck Grips

Part III. JIAN BU NA FA: Shoulder Grips

Part IV. XIOUNG LEI BEI BU NA FA: Countermeasures Against Grips from the Front, Flanks and the Rear

Part V. YAO FU BU NA FA: Counteractions Against Grips on the Waist and Stomach

Part VI. BI WAN BU NA FA: Grips on the Arm and Wrist

Part VII. SHOU ZHI BU: Grips on the Hand and Fingers

Part VIII. YIN TUI JIAO BU: Grips on the Genitalia, Legs and Feet

***

Synopsis of the Book

The book "CHIN NA FA"[1] was written by Liu Jin Sheng in collaboration with Zhao Jiang. The first edition of the book was issued in July of 1936 as a manual for the police academy of Zhejiang province. The book was printed by the publishing house Shan Wu in Shanghai. The book includes author's portrait, Zhao Jiang's preface (he is also known as Long Wen), introduction and description of the techniques CHIN NA with photos and detailed explanations. The techniques described can be conventionally grouped into eight parts. The first part is head holds[2]. The second part is neck holds. The third part is shoulders holds. The fourth part is front, side and back holds. The fifth side is torso and stomach holds. The sixth part is hand and wrist holds. The seventh part is fingers holds. The eighth part is genitals and legs holds. Great attention is also paid to counter-actions if the enemy tries to carry out some attacking action.

The author of the book, Liu Jin Sheng, was born in the province of Shandong. In his preface he writes: "In my childhood my grandfather (my mother's father) gave me an ancient manuscript book. I drilled during three years using pictures of the book and at that time I did not become aware of the true value of that book. Then I happened to learn under the guidance of the

---

Editor's notes:

[1] The hieroglyph CHIN in the title of the book means "catch" (noun), "catch" (verb), "grab" (noun), "grab" (verb), "seize" (verb); the hieroglyph NA means "hold" (noun), "hold" (verb), "grapple" (noun), "grapple" (verb), "grasp" (noun), "grasp (verb)", "grip" (noun), "grip" (verb), "control" (noun), "control" (verb); the hieroglyph FA means "skill", "method", "technique".
[2] The term "Hold" is used in this text as the most adequate translation of the hieroglyph "NA"; however, as mentioned above, the hieroglyph has a wider range of meaning. In this text it means not only a lock as such; it also means subsequent technical actions.

famous master of the North Wang Zi Ping[3] as well as over twenty other great masters. I drilled in various kinds of Martial Arts during more than twenty years. With certain experience behind me, I can say that the ancient manuscript preserved by my grandfather is priceless heritage of our National Martial Art."

Techniques of CHIN NA include a wide set of various movements: press and blows on vulnerable points, grappling, strangling, throws and so on. That set of movements (impacts on the enemy) allows to realize the following methods: "Separation (tearing) of muscles and sinews" (FENG JING), "Dislocating (breaking out) of bones and joints" (YU GU), "Suffocation" (BI QI) and "Impacting on points" (DIAN XUE). Also, those methods must be used skillfully, not just with brute force. Both army and police always attached great importance to this art.

The introduction to the book says: "Initially this skill had several names: FENG JING FA – "The technique of separation (breaking) of muscles and sinews"; DI TANG FA – "Methods of combat when lying on the ground"; YU GU FA – "The technique of dislocation (breaking out) of bones and joints" and CHIN NA FA – "The technique of seizing and grappling." At present the name CHIN NA FA has predominantly become established. Totally, there are 72 methods. The ancient manuscript calls this skill DI SHA SHOU – "Devil's Hand." Specialists in WU SHU say there are 36 "big" and 72 "small" points on a human body. 36 positions, 72 positions and 108 positions (techniques) are also marked out in CHIN NA FA.

Editor's notes:

[3] Wang Zi Ping (1881-1973) nicknamed Yon An, a Muslim from the town of Cangzhou in the province of Hebei. Was of a family of WU SHU masters. Trained from his childhood under the guidance of elder relatives. Later learnt HUA QUAN from Sha Bao Xing and Ma Yun Long, then CHA QUAN from Yang Hong Xu. In 1928, after foundation of the "Central Institute of National Martial Art" in Nanking, became the dean of the Shaolin faculty. One of outstanding masters of the XX century.

That traditional division has been maintained till now since long time when our ancestors created the theory of CHIN NA[4] on the basis of the conception 36 TIAN GANG[4] and 72 DI SHA[5]. But actually, that is only a tribute to tradition that has no great practical significance.

72 DI SHA - Spirits of 72 Stars

Preface by Zhao Jiang

Liu Jin Sheng xiansheng[6] learnt the martial art in the province of Shandong. He moved to the province of Zhejiang six years ago[7]. He has disciples all over the province. However, he lives a modest life, at his leisure time he exchanges views with his colleagues in the martial art. Long Wen is responsible for training the police of this province and realizes that policemen in their struggle against criminals can not conform to requirements without acquiring the martial art. Each time when we touch that topic to find quite quick as well as effective training methods, Liu xiansheng surely puts to the forefront CHIN NA. Our Martial Art (WU SHU) can cause body injuries to people, it is difficult to learn this art and reach perfection. When WU SHU is used, body damages are often done to people, but policemen are the people who protect public order. The best of all is to use method CHIN NA in order to subdue people instead of inflicting body damages to them. A good effect can be obtained with proper explanation and training. Now those who are responsible for public order will get this book to study it and use the art of CHIN NA in society's interests. It is for this purpose that we publish the book by Liu xiansheng.

Zhao Long Wen
March, 25-th of the Chinese Republic (1936)

Editor's notes:

[6] Xiansheng, a polite addressing to educated people, especially to older persons and teachers, in China, like Mr. or Sir in Britain.
[7] We wish to remind you that the book was published in 1936.

Preface by Liu Jin Sheng

Recently those who talk of military science mainly pay attention to various armaments of three branches of the armed forces (land forces, navy force and air force) and did not pay any attention to the national Martial Art (GUO SHU) inherent in China. After the defeat of I-He-Tuan followers[8] during the Qing dynasty[9], many believed that all who learnt WU SHU were bandits. WU SHU was held in bad repute because I-He-Tuan followers drilled in it. That's why people started to despise the national martial art.

Because of it men of matchless mastery in WU SHU are not in hurry to reveal their skill. Some of them even went for "knights of the road." As a consequence the Chinese nation was labeled as a "sick nation" and foreigners oppress us for a few decades.

Editor's notes:

[8] I-He-Tuan uprising, anti-Government uprising of peasants and poor town-dwellers in the northern China in 1899—1901. The uprising was initiated by the secret religious society I-He-Chuan ("The fist in the name of justice and concord"). Later insurgent troops were renamed to I-He-Tuan ("Detachments of justice and concord", hence the name of the uprising). As the name of society included the word Chuan, or Quan ("Fist") in recent standard spelling, foreigners called insurgents "boxers", which gave another name to the I-He-Chuan uprising – "Boxer Rebellion." The uprising started in the province of Shantung where particularly great influence of western powers and Christian missionaries felt. At the beginning of 1900 the center of the uprising moved to metropolitan province of Zhili. So-called "boxers" demolished railways and telegraph lines, buildings of religious missions and some governmental institutions, actually they exercised control over a vast territory. The movement spread to the provinces of Shansi and Manchuria. In 1901 the uprising was suppressed with active participation of troops from Western powers (Great Britain, Germany, Austria-Hungary, France, the USA, Russia, Italy) as well as Japan.
[9] The monarchic dynasty that ruled in China right until the Xinhai Revolution of 1911.

During several decades after Meiji Isin[10] Japan, our eastern neighbor, joined the ranks of leading world powers. Many think that it had happened as a result of imitation of Europe and West but they do not know that long before Meiji Ising the Japanese cultivated the spirit of samurais and Yamato[11]. Studies in so called "samurai spirit" showed that it originated in our country. During the Ming[12] dynasty some Chinese Chen Yuan Yun sailed to Japan and brought with him two kinds of the Chinese national martial art, in one of them grappling and throws prevailed. He taught local inhabitants who tried very hard and diligently acquired this skill. The Japanese government encouraged that activity and supported its development by all means. Finally, this kind of martial art was named Jujitsu and later Judo; it spread all over the country. The Japanese people educated in that atmosphere was becoming brave and militant.

Therefore, if we speak about the salvation of our Motherland, first of all we have to advocate our national martial art to keep up people's spirit. Although recently the central authorities following instructions of the prime-minister encourage exercises in national martial arts and both in the center and in provinces palaces of national martial art were founded, but besides wrestling, only two schools, Shaolin and Wudang, were noticeably spread. Also, individual training (mastering of forms, or TAO) is prevailed in those institutions but the applied aspect of techniques learnt is ignored. Therefore, if a man who has been exercising, say, even for twenty or thirty years and who engages a western boxer or a Japanese judo wrestler, will be surely defeated. Striving for nice-looking movements without

Editor's notes:

[10] MEIJI ISIN (means renovation, restoration of Meiji in Japanese), the revolution of 1867 - 1868 in Japan. It overthrew the power of seguns from the house of Tokugava and restored the power of emperors. The government headed by Mutsukhito (emperor Meiji) came to power, it took a path of social and economic reforms.

[11] YAMATO, a union of tribes in Japan in 3-4 centuries. On the base of this union the Japanese state was founded. The expression "Yamato spirit" became a synonym of the "Japanese spirit".

[12] The Ming dynasty ruled in China since 1368 till 1644.

practical use and absence of fighting spirit are at the bottom of it. In this way we shall lose little by little all the heritage of our ancestors who brilliantly used all methods and techniques in a combat. Now foreigners say with a touch of irony that the Chinese martial art is nothing else but a dance with energetic movements. Our ancestors knew how to drill by twos, one against another, and alone. They were able to employ various techniques one after another in a fight, attacking continuously the enemy so that he had no time to defend himself, nothing to say about fighting back. That is why such well-known generals of the Ming dynasty as Qi Jiguang, Yu Dayou and others encouraged a practical approach to training and rejected all showy and perfunctory things. They made a glorious mark in the history.

Today sciences develop, all branches of knowledge improve from day to day. Only our national martial art does not make any progress, moreover, it loses its secret methods, as our ancestors revealed their secrets very seldom. It is very pity. In my childhood my grandfather Fang Chen Xun gave me an ancient manuscript book. I drilled during three years using pictures of the book. At that time I did not become aware of the true value of that book. Then I happened to learn under the guidance of Wang Zi Ping, a famous master of the North, as well as over twenty other great masters. I drilled various kinds of Martial Arts during more than twenty years. With certain experience behind me, I can say that the ancient manuscript preserved by my grandfather is, indeed, priceless heritage of our National Martial Art. That's why I decided to publish this book for those who are sincerely eager to learn our national martial art.

Liu Jin Sheng
The Police Academy of Zhejiang Province
1-st of May of the 24-th year of the Chinese Republic (1935)

Explanations and Instructions

At first this art (skill) had several names: FENG JING FA – "The technique of separation (tearing) of muscles and sinews"; DI TANG FA – "Methods of combat when lying on the ground"; YU GU FA – "The technique of dislocating (breaking out) of bones and joints" and CHIN NA FA – "The technique of seizing and grappling." At present the name CHIN NA FA has predominantly become established. Totally, there are 72 methods. The ancient manuscript calls this skill DI SHA SHOU – "Devil's Hand." This secret technique perfectly suits both for self-defense and defense of Motherland. It is essential for training military men and policemen.

A very detailed description is supplied to each technique and method expounded in the book. The language is very simple in order everything to be understandable at first sight. All has been done to increase training efficiency at most.

This technique is exclusively designed for practical employment, not for decoration and show. When drilling alone, it is difficult to understand its wisdom to the end and catch all nuances. It is necessary to have sparring practice, really to oppose each other. Pain must be felt if touched, but too great effort must not be applied, otherwise a body damage – sprained muscles and sinews, bone fractures and etc. can be caused. It is as far as training sessions are concerned. However, you get quite another thing when it is a matter of life and death.

Each man who needs to master an effective system of self-defense, whoever he may be – civilian, military man or member of police, must have this book. It is necessary to systematically drill as shown in the photos and explained in the text. In the course of time everything will turn out all right. When you suddenly encounter an enemy and you have no firearms with you, you have to enter a hand-to-hand fight. If you mastered this skill (GONG FU), you will be able to win.

Moreover, having mastered this technique, you can sway the destiny of the enemy. If you are in command of this technique, you can kill your enemy, cause unbearable pain, tear his muscles and sinews, break his bones or make him unconscious for some time and completely disable him to resist.

When a criminal, being arrested, resists and shouts, a method of "temporary death" can be employed[13]. Or it is possible to grasp a certain part of his body and in such a way make him follow the escort. Then he can be "animated" again or his fixed extremity can be released. The duration of being in such a state must not exceed two hours.

Even a woman or a physically weak man who mastered this technique can curb a strong enemy. This technique demands deftness and skill, not brute force. It is necessary to train oneself daily to make the body flexible and nimble, but "hardness" must be hidden inside this "softness."

The men who perfect themselves in the Martial Art must drill methods of impacts on acupuncture points (DIAN XUE), blows (DA), grappling (NA), throws (SHUAI). Those four kinds of combat skillfully combined will mean matchless mastery. Depending on a situation, you can employ all four kinds of combat conduct, in that case even if you encounter a physically very strong enemy, you will win all the same. But to attain it, you must train yourself very seriously, be persistent and persevering.

Editor's notes:

[13] It implies that the enemy will be brought in unconscious state.

When men fight, they usually grapple each other. Under such conditions the employment of CHIN NA technique gives the best effect. It is necessary to pay special attention to it.

This method is very artful and effective. For a long time it was not passed (to other people) and was almost lost. Now we publish this rarity and pass the priceless Art to our compatriots as a gift.

People in our country know that the national martial art includes impact on points, grappling, throws, and blows. This book wholly deals with grappling (NA). Books on three other aspects of martial arts are being prepared for publication.

The book contains 99 photos. For the sake of better understanding complicated movements are disrupted into several parts and several photos, for example, photo 1, 2, 3 show intermediate phases of one continuous movement. The explanatory text is given for two opposing sides who are named "A" and "B". In case of a collective training session in the army or the police one rank acts as "A", another as "B".

When encountering an enemy, you must demonstrate courage, strength, mastery, and skill. You mast act by surprise, move swiftly, in that case you will win. The most important thing is not to lose heart. If you lost heart, you will lose everything.

SHAOLIN CHIN NA

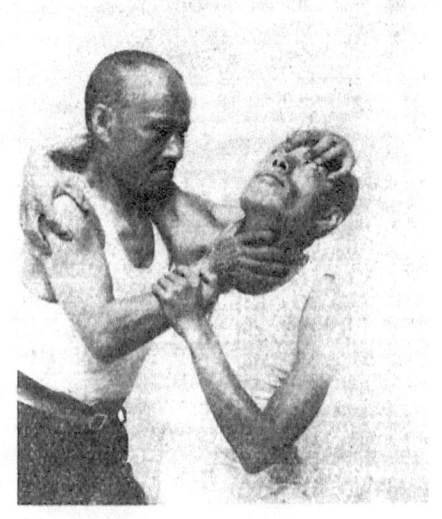

Part I.

TOU BU NA FA
Head Grips

During the period of dynasty MING and later in the beginning of dynasty QING[14] people's hair was laid in a knot. At that time methods of seizing by hair considered in paragraph one and two were used rather often: really, if somebody strongly seizes by the hair near the roots, it is difficult to get free.

Modern people also have hair but it is not laid in a knot. Therefore, if one's hair is rather long, the enemy can seize the hair near the roots at once, and if the hair is short, it is not always possible to do, at any rate, a seizure will be not so strong. It should be taken into consideration when using those methods and make required corrections. However, the technique of effecting on an enemy's wrist which makes a grip mainly remains the same.

A long time ago everybody had long hair, that's why the book contains such paragraphs. At our time living conditions have changed, everybody is closely cropped or has his hair cut short, one is not able of seizing by the hair. This manuscript was written in ancient times and we decided to leave as it is, without deleting anything.

Paragraph 1. QIAN ZHUA FA: Seizure by the hair from the front (variant 1).

This method is employed if the enemy standing in front of you seized you by the hair on the top of your head.

Editor's notes:

[14] The Ming dynasty ruled in China since 1368 till 1644, then the power passed to the Qing dynasty that ruled until Xinhai Revolution of 1911.

Photo 1 – "Seizure by the hair from the front" (variant 1).

Explanations

B(A) has seized A(B) from the front with his right (left) hand by the hair. A(B) must quickly cover the enemy's hand that is making a seizure with both palms, press it to his head and pull it back with force. At the same time the torso and the head must move back[15] so that the enemy's arm making a seizure by the hair will straighten in the elbow joint but its wrist will remain slightly bent[16]. At that instant it is necessary abruptly draw (bend) forward with the whole body, press as strong as possible with the head and the hands (on an enemy's hand) a little bit to the right (left) and downward. It is necessary to abruptly press with palms[17] on the enemy's hand at the point which lies one CUN[18] below the wrist on its outer side. A fracture of the wrist will occur. **Photo 1 – "Seizure by the hair from the front" (variant 1).**

Editor's notes:

[15] For that purpose "A" must make a small step backward and slightly bend back in his waist.
[16] For that purpose it is necessary to lower the chin to the breast.
[17] "To chop" in the original text.
[18] CUN, a Chinese unit of length, equal to about 3.33 cm, or 1.312 inches.

Paragraph 2. QIAN ZHUA FA: Seizure by the hair from the front (variant 2).

This method is not a vital one for the people of today with their hair shortly cut or with a shaven head like that one of the author of this book.

This method is employed when the enemy, as in the first case, standing in the front, seized you by the hair on the top of your head.

Photo 2 – "Seizure by the hair from the front" (variant 2).

Explanations

As in the first case, B(A) has seized A(B) with his right (left) hand by the hair. It is necessary to cover the hand of the enemy with the right (left) palm and tightly press it to your head, the middle finger being thrust under his palm. At the same time you seize with the left (right) hand the enemy's arm from above 2 or 3 CUNs[19] above the wrist, move the body and the head back so that his arm is straightened in the elbow joint and the wrist a little bit bent. At that instant it is necessary to stoop down abruptly, at the same time the left (right) leg makes a step forward, the left (right) elbow pressing on the enemy's arm from above downward and forward. This movement must be fast and strong, in that case a wrist fracture will occur. **Photo 2 – "Seizure by the hair from the front" (variant 2).**

Paragraph 3. HOU ZHUA FA: Seizure by the hair from behind.

This method is very effective but when it is employed, it is necessary to take into account difference in height and build. Let's consider a case when a man, small and relatively weak from physical point of view, encountered an enemy who is a head taller and substantially stronger. In this case the small weak man, even if he takes the position shown in photo 3, can not overpower the enemy. Here some additional actions are required, for instance, it is possible to deliver an elbow blow on his ribs or stoop and strike at his genitalia. After that action the above method can be successfully used.

This method is used if the enemy standing behind seized you by the hair on the back of your head.

Editor's notes:

[19] 6.6-9.9 cm, or 2.6-3.9 in.

Explanations

B(A), standing behind the back of A(B), has seized his hair with the right (left) hand. A(B) must quickly cover the enemy's hand with his right (left) palm, press it to the back of his head with force and slightly move with his whole torso to the right (left), pulling the enemy with himself, and at the same time he must turn to the left (right) by 90 degrees. It is necessary "to prop up", from below upward, the tip of the enemy's elbow with

Photo 3 – "Seizure by the hair from behind."

the left (right) palm and at the same time to bend the body to the right (left) to have the enemy's caught arm straightened in the elbow joint and the head slightly tossed back to turn the enemy's caught arm with the elbow down. Press on the enemy's elbow joint against its natural bend with the left (right) arm from below upward, that will make the enemy draw himself up and stand on tiptoe. If a movement is made abruptly and with sufficient effort, a fracture of the elbow joint will occur. **Photo 3 – "Seizure by the hair from behind."**

Paragraph 4. DUAN DENG: Clasping a lamp.

It is very effective, though relatively dangerous (for your opponent) method. After becoming unconscious from violent pain the enemy goes into a coma, a man, being in this state for a long time, can die. Therefore, it is necessary to know methods which can help him to go out of that state. To employ that method effectively, one must have strong arms, specially trained fingers, otherwise it will be to no purpose. When executing that method the second arm performs an auxiliary function.

This method is applicable to an enemy in any position - standing, sitting or lying one.

Explanations

A(B) seizes the lobe of the left (right) ear of the enemy with his right (left) thumb and forefinger, his right (left) middle finger presses with force on the tendon below the ear and a little bit above protruding bone (angle) of the lower jaw where the point of "muscle numbness" lies. It is necessary to press inward and a little upward. At the same time you must seize the right (left) part of the enemy's head above the temple with your left (right)

Photo 4 – "Clasping a lamp."

hand and press to the right (left) and downward with force. Press at the same time with both hands to squeeze the enemy's head as strong as possible. If everything has been done properly, the enemy's body grows numb immediately and he will become unconscious from violent pain. It needs long drilling to make fingers strong, otherwise it is difficult to get required effect[20]. **Photo 4 – "Clasping a lamp."**

Paragraph 5. ZHUA LIAN: Seizing by the face.

Photo 5 shows how to seize the enemy's hand properly: it is necessary to seize and squeeze his thumb with your little finger and the fourth finger and press his hand to your chest with your palm. Grip and control of the enemy's thumb is a key to effective employment of this method.

After execution of protective actions it is necessary to counterattack without delay, otherwise there is a risk of exposing your head to a blow.

Point QU CHI:

曲池穴

This method is employed when the enemy is downright in front of you and he is pushing you on your breast or seizing your clothes.

Editor's notes:

[20] Training methods for fingers are described in detail in the book by Jin Jing Zhong "Authentic Shaolin Heritage: Training Methods of 72 Arts of Shaolin" (Tanjin, 1934) ISBN: 978-1847284068 / www.kungfulibrary.com /

Explanations

B(A) reaches out his right (left) arm with the aim to push or seize by the clothes on the breast of A(B). A(B) must immediately cover the hand of the B(A) with his left (right) hand, slightly "draw in" his chest, shift backward a little with the whole torso, and tightly press the enemy's hand to his breast.

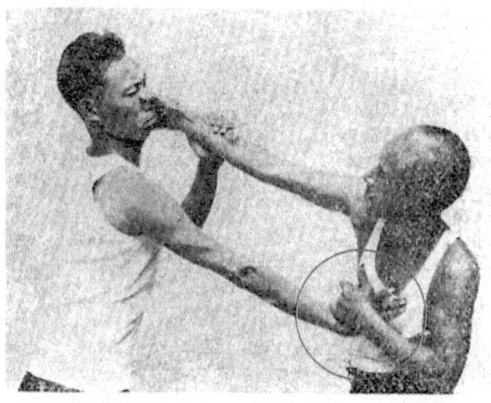

Photo 5 – "Seizing by the face."

Concurrently with that movement of the right (left) hand deliver fast and strong blow from above downward to the region of the point QU CHI that lies on the side of elbow bent, which will cause reflex bending of the enemy's arm. You use it and immediately approach the enemy, at that the right (left) hand moves forward and upward without stopping and seizes the enemy by the face: the thumb props up against the bridge of the nose from its right (left) side and the other four fingers press with force on the tendon under the left (right) ear, a little bit above the protruding angle of the lower jaw in the region of the point of "muscle numbness". Pressing must be done with force, in that case all muscles of the enemy will numb and he will not be able to move an arm or leg. Actions must be well coordinated and fast when using this method. **Photo 5 – "Seizing by the face."**

Paragraph 6. ZHAI KUI: Taking off the helmet.

When you employ this method, it is necessary to act resolutely and fast, otherwise the enemy can break away.

The method is used when the enemy tries to wring your neck.

Explanations

A(B) seizes B(A) by the hair on the back of the enemy's head with his right (left) hand, concurrently he props up against his chin on the left side with the left (right) hand, at that the elbow of the right (left) arm of the A(B) in a bent position must prop up against

Photo 6 – "Taking off the helmet", first phase.

the enemy's chest below the armpit to form a lever for the right (left) arm. The right (left) hand pulls the hair seized at the back of the head toward itself and downward and the left (right) hand pushes the enemy's chin from itself and upward. When you execute the method, you must tightly lean with your right (left) side against the left (right) side of the enemy body as to his left (right) arm to remain behind your back. It is to avoid such possible enemy's counteractions as a seizure and pressing your genitalia. **It is the first phase of the method "Taking off the helmet", photo 6.**

It is a very important moment: it is possible to avoid a grip and carry out a countermeasure only at the very beginning of actions of the enemy when he has not applied all his force yet.

The second phase:

Let's consider further a possible countermeasure against the method "Taking off the helmet". Let us assume that B(A) tries to employ the method "Taking off the helmet" against A(B) but he has not applied the utmost effort yet. A(B) must instantly bring his right (left) arm back, cover the hand that seized him by the hair and firmly press it to the back of his head. Simultaneously it is necessary to move the

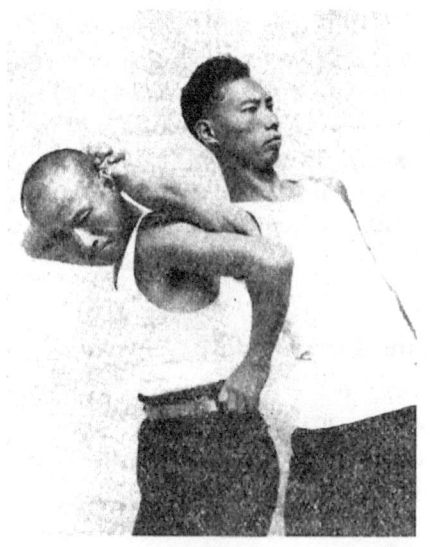

Photo 7 – "Taking off the helmet", second phase.

body a little bit back by bending in the waist, squat partly to lower the left (right) shoulder to the level of the right (left) elbow of the enemy's arm which seized the hair, push that elbow with your shoulder to the right (left), then "prop up" (the elbow) upward. In the course of those actions the body will turn to the right (left) by 180 degrees. Due to it the arm of the enemy that pushes the chin loses its force, as the head turns to the pushing side. It is necessary to pull with the right (left) arm to the right (left) and downward with force. At the same time you should "prop up" (the enemy's elbow) with your left (right) shoulder and elbow upward, the whole body will also rise a little up. Those actions will result in a fracture of the elbow joint of the enemy. **It is the second phase of the method "Taking off the helmet", photo 7.**

If you failed to break the elbow, it is necessary to proceed immediately to the third phase of this method, as described below.

Explanations to photo 8: As mentioned above, advantage in body height and strength is an important factor that must be always taken into account. In photo 8 one of opponents is significantly taller and he can use this advantage. If he turns to the right and at the same time pushes off the elbow that "props up" his right arm with his left palm, he will be able to avoid a grip and get free himself. Besides, he will find himself behind the back of his enemy and will be able to use that position for taking countermeasures.

The third phase:

Let's consider a possible continuation of the second phase of the method: A(B) turns to the right (left) with the aim of "propping up" with the shoulder the enemy's arm that is held. At that moment B(A) started to counteract with the aim to get free himself from the grip. A(B) must push upward with the left elbow with a concurrent abrupt turn of the whole

Photo 8 – "Taking off the helmet", third phase.

body to the right (left) as to remain to be back to back with the enemy. At that the right (left) hand of the A(B) must firmly hold the enemy's hand that seized him by the hair, the head and the whole body must be bent down. In that position it is extremely difficult for the enemy to get himself free. The left arm, if necessary, intensifies actions of the right arm by catching the enemy's held arm near the wrist. Make a strong pull forward and downward and a fracture of the elbow joint will occur. **It is the third phase of the method "Taking off the helmet", photo 8.**

Paragraph 7. PU SHU: Catching a mouse.

To employ effectively this method, it is necessary to have sufficiently strong fingers.

The method is employed when the enemy attacks from the front and tries to grapple your torso with his arms or to seize you by your waist belt.

Photo 9 – "Catching a mouse."

Explanations

B(A) attacks A(B) from the front and tries to grapple his torso with one or two arms or seize by his waist belt. A(B) must immediately retreat, at the same time pull the enemy to himself to make him lean forward. At that moment B(A) can use the situation in his favor and butt, therefore it is necessary to act fast. A(B) must raise up his hands and seize the enemy for his cheeks from both sides, pressing at that with his fingers on tendons below the ears with force. He must do his best to thrust his fingers as deep as possible and pull toward himself, at that moving with the whole body back. Muscles of the enemy's whole body will numb and he will not be able to move with an arm or a leg. **See photo 9 - "Catching a mouse."**

Paragraph 8. AN TOU DUAN JING: Pressing on head and breaking neck.

Two men showing methods in photos 10 and 11 have a noticeable difference in height. Whether it was done deliberately or happened by chance, but at any rate it reminds us once more that it is necessary to take into account height, build and physical strength of the enemy when using any technique in practice. Surely it does not mean that a man of small height always loses, not at all. As a rule, men of small height are more deft and move faster but it is necessary to have sufficiently high level of skill to use this advantage. For example, in photo 10 the difference in height is by a head. It will not be a simple task for the man whose height is lower to "cover" the eyes of the enemy from behind. The same situation is shown in photo 11: although the partner of small height has carried out a grip but he himself already staggers. If the level of skill is not sufficiently high, that position is quite dangerous for him.

The method is employed when the enemy attacks from the front, moving forward resolutely.

Explanations

B(A) attacks and punches with the right (left) fist. A(B) slightly leans his torso to the right (left) and dodges the punch, at that he deflects the striking arm of the enemy to the left (right) with the right (left) hand. Simultaneously the left leg of A(B) makes a step toward the enemy and the left (right) side of his chest sets against the right (left) side of the enemy. At that moment A(B)

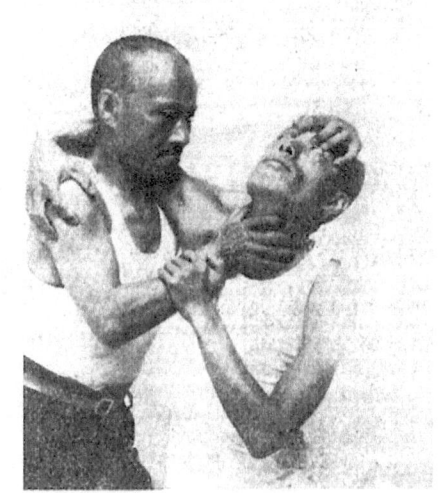

Photo 10 – "Pressing on head and breaking neck".

pushes the enemy's chin with his right (left) hand from below upward and forward and supports the back of the enemy from behind with the left (right) forearm and elbow to prevent the enemy from falling back. Then, move immediately the left (right) hand upward and forward and hook the upper edges of the enemy's eye-sockets with the forefinger and the fourth finger bent like a hook. It is necessary to pull back and down with force to make him bend back. If at that moment both arms apply an abrupt effort, there will occur a fracture of the neck. If the chance is missed, the enemy can try to dodge back and avoid a grip. In that case it is necessary instantly to change the method for another one depending on the situation. In a word, if you failed to carry out the method, you should immediately change for another one and you will succeed. **See photo 10: "Pressing on head and breaking neck."**

Paragraph 9. AN TIAN GU: Pressing on the celestial drum.

The method is usually employed against a physically strong enemy. To carry it out, it is necessary to be behind the back of the enemy.

Explanations

B(A) goes or seats. A(B), catching the moment, appears behind his back. It is necessary to thrust through both arms under the enemy's arm-pits, raise them up to the point TIAN GU[21], seize the wrist of the other hand with one hand and press forward and downward with force. At that, it is necessary to try to keep the hands higher, incline the upper part of the torso back and stick out the stomach forward. In that

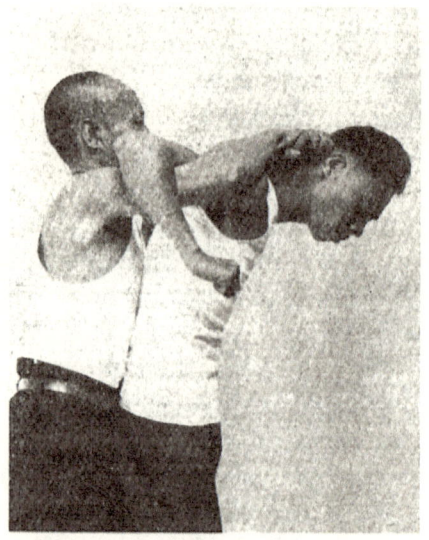

Photo 11 – "Pressing on the celestial drum."

case the enemy will stagger and it will be very difficult for him to get himself free. If you press with the arms down with force, the enemy feels sharp pain in the neck and vertigo appears and due to it he loses his ability to resist. If the enemy tries to use the countermeasure called "Falling on the ground, making a somersault to free himself", at no events must you let him off. It is necessary to fall with him to the ground without loosening the grip and go on pressing with arms as to cause displacement of his neck vertebrae. **See photo 11 - "Pressing on the celestial drum."**

Editor's notes:

[21] The point TIAN GU is located on the base of the skull vault, above the point of connection of the skull vault and the neck section of the spine.

SHAOLIN CHIN NA

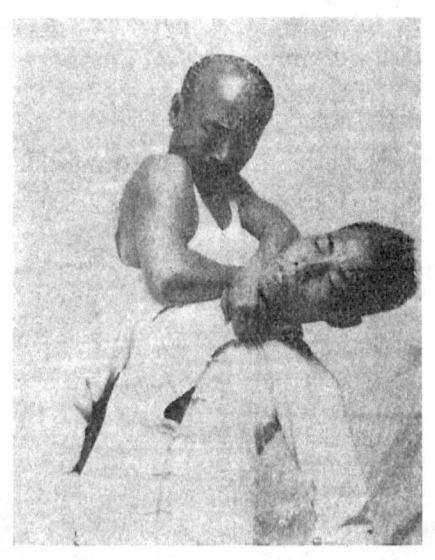

Part II.

JING BU NA FA
Neck Grips

Paragraph 1. NIE SU: Squeezing the crop.

One of WU SHU proverbs says: "If you have strength, go straight forward, no strength – go from a side". It means the following: to attack the enemy frontally, it is necessary to have not only a higher level of skill but good physical conditions (a well-trained body) as well.

The method is employed in case of a frontal attack of the enemy if he punches or tries to seize by the head.

Explanations

B(A) resolutely reduces the distance and punches with his right (left) fist, moving toward A(B). A (B) turns the attacking arm of the enemy with the right (left) hand to the left (right), simultaneously he makes a step forward as to his left (right) shoulder to set against an arm-pit of the enemy. At that, the arm which made a blow finds itself above his left (right) shoulder. It is necessary to put your left (right) arm round the enemy's

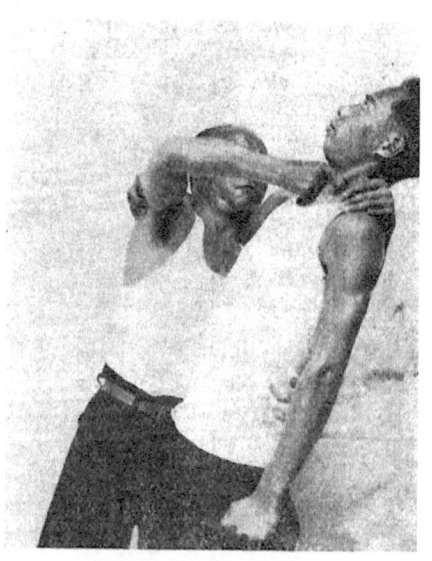

Photo 12 – "Squeezing the crop."

shoulders, seize his left (right) shoulder with the left (right) hand, abruptly make a pull to you and immediately from you. At that moment squeeze his gullet with the right (left) thumb and forefinger and press on his Adam's apple with the bent middle finger. The enemy will not be able to breathe and become unconscious from suffocation soon. **See photo 12 - "Squeezing the crop."**

Paragraph 2. JIAN JIA BO: Squeezing with arms from the front.

As a rule, WU SHU masters seldom use such a technique as head butts. However, when you are very close to the enemy or there are evident flaws and faults in his actions, it is quite possible to strike at him with a shoulder or the head.

The method is employed if the enemy butts you with his head in the region of the chest or tries, after bending, to execute a grip of the lower part of your body.

Explanations

B(A) butts at the chest of A(B). A(B) moves his arms to sides a little, at the same time he dodges to the left (right) and an enemy's blow gets to the void. Then he quickly steps forward, bends a little, tightly grapples and squeezes the neck of the attacking enemy with his right (left) arm. At that, it is necessary to squeeze (block) arteries on the left side of the enemy's neck with the elbow bend and the arteries on the right side of his neck with the forearm of the same arm. Seize the wrist of your own right (left) arm with the left (right) hand. Strongly squeeze the enemy's neck, straighten your back and slightly move your torso back.

As one can see from photo 13, B's shoulder is at the level of the solar plexus of A. Therefore, if A actions are not resolutely enough or his grip is not strong enough, B can deliver a blow at his solar plexus with an abrupt movement of the shoulder. Besides, B can deliver an elbow blow at A's left side. A possibility of these countermeasures should be taken into account.

If arteries are squeezed in such a way, a man can die within three seconds. It is necessary to exert an effect on the point FAN YAN for reanimation but it needs a certain qualification, that's why it is better not to bring to the fatal outcome. If the enemy attacks you with a great drive and knocks you down, never loosen your grip. It is necessary to grapple his torso with your legs and pull from you with force, squeezing his neck with arms until he loses his ability to resist. **Photo 13 – "Squeezing with arms from the front."**

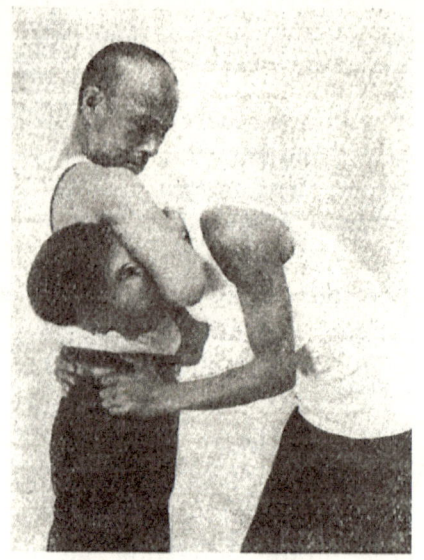

Photo 13 – "Squeezing with arms from the front."

Paragraph 3. HOU JIA BO: Squeezing with arms from behind.

This method can be used against an ordinary man who is not specially trained. However, if opponents are equal in strength and skill, it is difficult to succeed.

This method is used for arresting a dangerous criminal to prevent possible resistance or in hand-to-hand fighting when one succeeds in getting behind the back of the enemy. This method results in "temporary death".

Explanations

A(B) sees B(A) who is in a sitting or standing position and does not expect an attack. It is necessary to appear inconspicuously behind his back, grapple his neck from the front with the left (right) arm and pull back (toward oneself), raise immediately the right (left) arm bent in elbow, seize firmly by the right (left) biceps with the left (right) hand, press the right (left) palm to the enemy's back of the head in the region of the

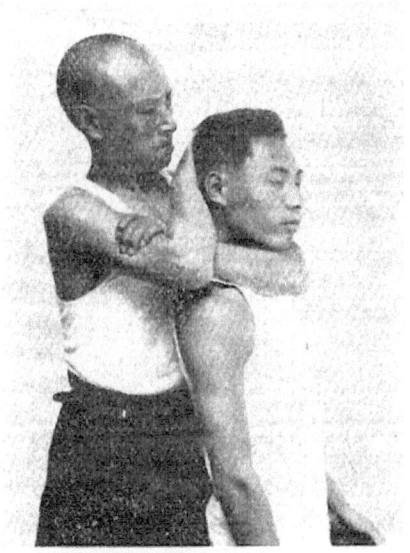

Photo 14 – "Squeezing with arms from behind."

point TIAN GU and press forward with force. The left (right) arm must be bent in elbow with force, it will cut off the neck arteries, blood flow will stop there and the man will die in three seconds. Therefore, before using this method, the technique of effecting the point FAN YANG must be acquired well, it is possible to reanimate a man and save him from death only by effecting that point. **Photo 14 - "Squeezing with arms from behind."**

Paragraph 4. QIANG SUO HOU: Pinching (blocking) the throat from the front.

It is necessary to pay attention to the following: this method should be used either in case when the enemy does not expect an attack or when the detention is carried out by a group of several men and during hand-to-hand fighting they succeeded in knocking the criminal down to the ground.

This method is used when in the course of hand-to-hand fighting you succeeded in toppling the enemy or when he is initially in a sitting or lying position and does not expect an attack.

Explanations

A and B are engaged in hand-to-hand fighting and in the course of it B(A) fell down on the ground. A(B) must quickly spring down to the fallen enemy, squeeze him with thighs from sides in the region of the waist, weigh down on his neck from above with his left or right forearm and press his head to the ground.

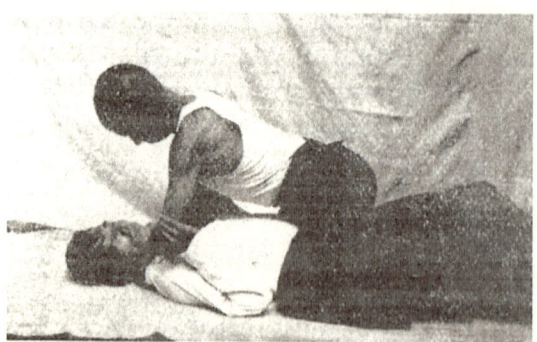

Photo 15 – "Pinching (blocking) the throat from the front."

At that moment it is necessary to thrust your right (left) hand into the lapel of the enemy's clothes and seize the right (left) side of his collar, in a similar way - the left side of his collar with your left hand. It is important that both hands should firmly seize the enemy's collar crosswise, then it is necessary to pull to the left and right with force. B(A) will die within three seconds. It is necessary to exert an effect on the point FAN YANG for reanimation. During practice sessions it is necessary to execute this method very carefully, without any effort. **Photo 15 – "Pinching (blocking) the throat from the front."**

Paragraph 5. HOU SUO HOU: Pinching (blocking) the throat from behind.

Conditions of the employment of this method is similar to the previous one: either in case when a criminal does not expect an attack or in case when the detention is carried out by a group of several men and during hand-to-hand fighting they succeeded in toppling the criminal down to the ground.

This method is used either in a right moment of a hand-to-hand struggle or if initially the enemy is in a sitting position and does not expect an attack.

Explanations

B(A) sits on the ground or is engaged in hand-to-hand fighting with A(B). Choosing a right moment, A(B) must get to the right (left) side of B(A), thrust his left (right) hand into the lapel of the enemy's clothes with a quick movement and catch the left (right) side of his collar. The left (right) hand must thrust into the lapel of the enemy's clothes with the palm in position "outside" and seize the collar from "inside". Then immediately the right (left) hand with the palm down must push through under your own left (right) arm and seize the enemy by his clothes in the region of the shoulder near the neck, a little bit closer to the shoulder-blade. It turns out to be a cross-wise arm grip.

- 43 -

Make one step to the left (right) and move to get behind the back of the enemy. Pull with both arms to opposite sides, the left hand being turned with the palm "inside" (toward the enemy) and the breast being stuck out forward. In that position the left (right) side of the enemy's collar cuts off (blocks) the arteries on the left (right) side of his neck and the side of the right (left) forearm with a spot located 2 or 3 CUNs[22] above the wrist cuts off

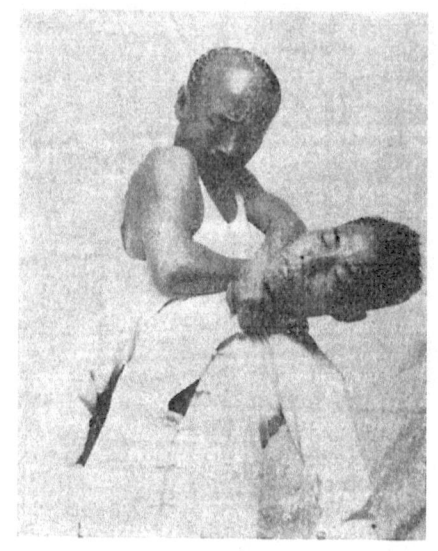

Photo 16 – "Pinching the throat from behind."

(blocks) the arteries on the right (left) side of his neck. It results in loss of the ability to resist and death of the enemy. It is necessary to exert an effect on the point FAN YANG for reanimation. This method must not be used with force during practice sessions. It is necessary to be especially careful if your partner suffers from pulmonary diseases. **Photo 16 - "Pinching the throat from behind."**

Editor's notes:

[22]6.6-9.9 cm, or 2.6-3.9 in.

Paragraph 6. BIE SHOU FENG HOU: Blocking an arm and pinching the throat.

This method is aimed at blocking blood vessels that feed the brain. Therefore, it must not be used without good reason.

The method is used when a criminal is arrested to avoid noise or possible resistance. In such a state the criminal can be brought to a required place and reanimated there. The duration of "temporary death" must not exceed two hours.

Explanations

A(B), seizing an opportunity, catches B(A) for the left side of his collar with the right (left) hand with the thumb thrusting behind the lapel of the collar and four other fingers squeezing the collar from outside. After catching the collar, it is necessary to get immediately to some place behind the back of the enemy, thrust your left (right) hand under his left (right) armpit, raise your hand up, lean against the enemy's neck with a side of the forearm

Photo 17 – "Blocking an arm and pinching the throat."

near the wrist and press with the elbow up with force. Those actions will result in raising the left (right) arm of B(A) above the left (right) shoulder of A(B). In that position the right (left) hand of A(B) pulls by the collar back (toward itself), because of it the left (right) side of the enemy's collar pinches the artery on the left (right) side of his neck. At the same time the left (right) arm of A(B) presses forward and downward and blocks the right artery with the side of the palm. The enemy becomes unconscious within three seconds as a consequence of the

- 45 -

disorder of blood circulation in his brain. For reanimation the point FAN YANG must be effected. It is necessary to acquire well the reanimating technique, otherwise it is not recommended to drive the situation to a loss of consciousness. **Photo 17 - "Blocking an arm and pinching the throat."**

Paragraph 7. LE JING DUAN BI: Squeezing the neck and breaking an arm.

This method is used if in the course of hand-to-hand fighting the enemy fell down to the ground. Two variants of executing the method are possible. In the first case the neck of the enemy is squeezed, that leads to loss of consciousness and death. In the second case pressure is exerted on the arm, that leads to its fracture.

Explanations

Let's assume that in the course of hand-to-hand fighting B(A) falls down to the ground with his face down (it is of no importance if he did it on purpose or the fall was caused by enemy's actions).

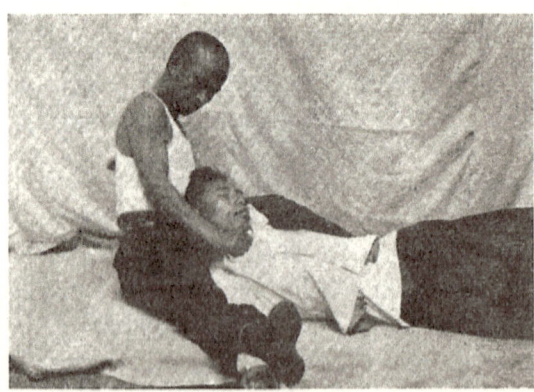

Photo 18 - "Squeezing the neck and breaking an arm."

Without delay A(B) must rush to him from above and to press his head to the ground with the breast, thrust the left (right) arm under the armpit of the left (right) arm of the enemy from below, press with the forearm up, move the left (right) hand to the right and forward above the left (right) shoulder of the enemy and seize the right (left) part of his collar. As a result of those actions the left (right) arm of B(A) becomes blocked with the left (right) arm of A(B). Concurrently with those actions the right (left) hand of A(B) seizes the left (right) part of the enemy collar from the front. After the enemy collar is firmly seized cross-wise it is necessary to pull to the right (left) and back with force and at the same time roll (turn over) to the right (left) with the face up. At that press the right (left) arm of the enemy to the ground with your right (left) leg and press on the left (right) elbow of the enemy from below with your left (right) thigh. In that position B(A) can not free himself: if he tries to turn to the left (right), the collar squeezes his neck, that will lead to asphyxia and the stoppage of blood circulation; if he tries to turn to the right (left), his elbow joint, being in a critical position, will certainly fracture. In that position it will be enough for A(B) to make a slight effort and the left (right) elbow of B(A) will be fractured. **Photo 18 - "Squeezing the neck and breaking an arm."**

Paragraph 8. JIAO JING: Grappling the neck obliquely.

The method is used if during hand-to-hand fighting enemies fall down to the ground or if since the start the enemy is in a sitting or lying position.

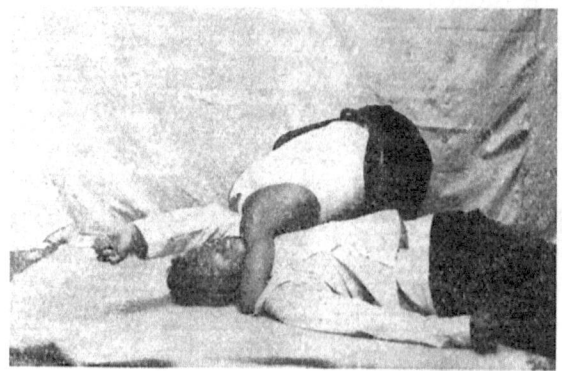

Photo 19 - "Grappling the neck obliquely."

Explanations

In the course of a combat B(A) falls flat on his back. A(B) instantly rushes to his left (right) side, puts left (right) arm round the enemy's neck, at the same time pushes the enemy's left (right) arm with the right (left) arm and draws it aside and upward, thrusting head under the enemy's shoulder. As a result of it the left (right) arm of the enemy will be firmly squeezed (fixed) between the left (right) shoulder of A(B) and his head. Then it is necessary to seize firmly the wrist of the left (right) arm with the right (left) hand and squeeze the enemy with force. During those actions the left (right) leg is bent, the right (left) leg is straightened to a side and the foot is planted firmly to maintain stability. In that position the left shoulder of A(B) pinches the left artery on the enemy's neck and the lower part of his right forearm near the wrist pinches the right artery. Within three seconds breathing and blood circulation of B(A) stop. For reanimation the point FAN YANG must be effected. **Photo 19 - "Grappling the neck obliquely."**

SHAOLIN CHIN NA

Part III.

JIAN BU NA FA
Shoulder Grips

Paragraph 1. DAO BI XIE JIAN: Pressing an arm, dislocating a shoulder.

The sketch shows the direction of pressure on the wrist during an initial phase of the method. As a result of it the enemy will be forced to fall dawn to the ground.

The method is used to arrest a criminal and allows to avoid possible resistance.

Photo 20 - "Pressing an arm, dislocating a shoulder."

Explanations

B(A) walks and does not expect an attack, A(B) walks toward him. Arms of both men are down as it is usual done during a walk. A(B), after coming up to B(A), instantly seizure his left (right) hand with the left (right) hand. It is necessary to seize from behind in order the thumb to be on the back of the hand and other four fingers on the side of the palm. After seizing firmly the enemy's hand one must raise it abruptly up and to a side. Immediately the right (left) arm helps the left (right) one seizing the enemy's hand in the same manner. As a result of it two thumbs press outward (from itself) and other fingers inward (to itself). At the same time it is necessary to press on the enemy's hand downward and forward so that his wrist would be bent. Pull the enemy to you, then abruptly push him forward and downward and he is bound to fall dawn. Your right (left) foot steps on the left (right) shoulder of the enemy, that will make him press his whole body to the ground. After that bring the held arm of the enemy behind his back with both arms, move the right (left) foot to a little lower and press the upper part of the enemy's arm to the ground and prop up his forearm with the front part of your shin. It is necessary to tread down and forward strongly and press forward with your shin. In that position the whole body of B(A), his arms and legs are immovable, but the arms of A(B) are free, he can take a cord or a belt and tie up the enemy. If a necessity appears, for instance, under the threat of an attack of accomplices, it is possible to move a leg forward abruptly and a dislocation of the shoulder will occur. **Photo 20 - "Pressing an arm, dislocating a shoulder."**

Paragraph 2. KOU ZHOU: Pressing on an elbow.

It should be pointed out that a kick at a knee is more effective than that one at a pelvic bone and it is more difficult to ward it off. In any case coordinated actions of arms and legs need a good degree of training, otherwise one can not overwhelm one's enemy.

This method is employed if the enemy seized you by your clothes in the shoulder region.

Explanations

B(A) seizes A(B) by his clothes in the region of the right (left) shoulder with the left (right) hand. A(B) immediately covers the upper part of the enemy's forearm with both hands, the fingers of his hands being crossed. A(B) pulls the arm of the enemy to him with concurrent downward pressure so that the enemy could not turn and slip out. Simultaneously he presses on

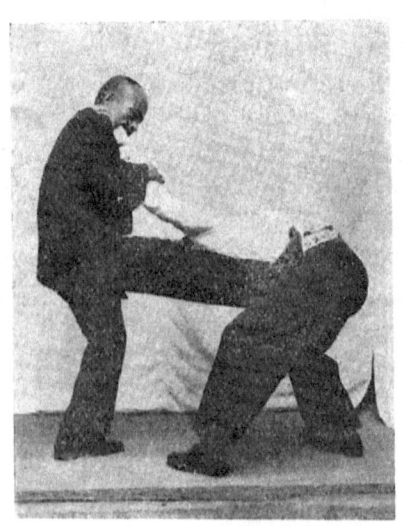

Photo 21 – "Pressing on an elbow."

the left (right) pelvic bone of the enemy with the sole of the right (left) foot. A coordinated effort of arms and a leg will lead to a fracture of the elbow. **Photo 21 - "Pressing on an elbow."**

- 52 -

Paragraph 3. ZHUA JIAN: Gripping by a shoulder.

This method can be successfully used against ordinary people who did not go through special training. As a result a fracture of a wrist or an elbow is possible. However, it is easier to succeed in fracturing an elbow.

This method is used if the enemy, as in the previous case, seized you by your clothes in the shoulder region.

Explanations

B(A) seized A(B) by the clothes in the region of the right (left) shoulder with left (right) hand. A(B) instantly covers the hand of the enemy with his left (right) hand and firmly presses it to his shoulder. It is necessary to firmly press the seized hand of the enemy, make a step back to have his arm straightened and immediately make a step forward and to the left to turn the held arm with its elbow outside. At that moment one must continue to execute the method as described below. **Photo 22: the first phase of the method "Gripping by a shoulder."**

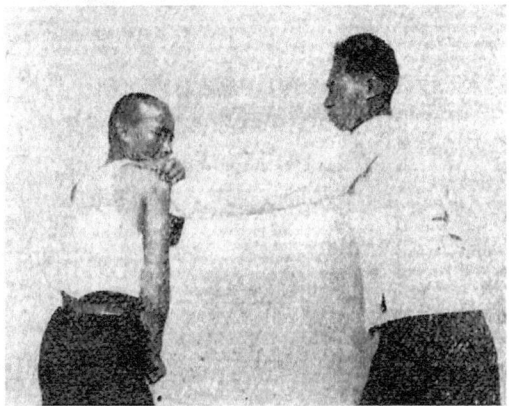

Photo 22 - "Gripping by a shoulder", first phase.

Continuation

A(B) makes a step with the right (left) leg to the left (right), his right (left) shoulder and the whole torso turns to the left (right). It is necessary to use "twisting" force of the waist. Simultaneously his right (left) arm moves back, then rises up from below and from above presses down on the held arm of the enemy a little higher than the elbow. During a turn of the torso to the left (right) the held hand of the enemy must be firmly pressed to the shoulder so that he feels some pain in the wrist. As a consequence of those actions B(A) will be forced to kneel down on the right (left) knee and lean on the ground with the right (left) arm. In that position B(A) loses the ability to resist. If pressed strongly, a fracture of the wrist will occur. **Photo 23: The second phase of the method "Gripping by a shoulder."**

Photo 23 - "Gripping by a shoulder", second phase.

Paragraph 4. BAU ZHOU: Squeezing an elbow.

We repeat once again that one needs experience, exactness of movements, and force to get success, without them the best method will yield no result.

This technique is used if the course of executing the previous method "Gripping a shoulder" the enemy tries to slip out and free himself from a grip.

Photo 24 - "Squeezing an elbow."

Explanations

In the course of executing the previous method (paragraph 3, "Gripping by a shoulder") A(B) turns his torso to the left, trying to straighten the held arm of the enemy and turn it so that the elbow will be outside. However, B(A) prevents him from doing so and follows A(B) on a circle in the same direction. In that case A(B) must instantly proceed to the technique "Pressing with a turn" without losing control over the left (right) arm of the enemy. For that it is necessary to make a step with the right (left) leg forward and not allow the enemy to increase distance, thrust the right (left) hand under the armpit of the left (right) arm of the enemy and seize him by the shoulder from behind, stretch the left (right) arm forward past the left (right) cheek of the enemy, bend the wrist and "catch" his neck with the hand in the shape of a hook from the rear. Both arms press down as strong as possible to make the enemy bend forward and lean on the ground with the right (left) hand, his left (right) arm being raised up and being "supported" with your right (left) shoulder. At that moment it is necessary to bend the right (left) arm in elbow at a right angle and press with the forearm in the region of the crook of the arm on the left (right) arm of the enemy. It is necessary to press on the bone of upper arm near the elbow. Concurrently squeeze the wrist of your right (left) arm with the left (right) hand, pull to you with force and straighten your back. A fracture of the enemy's arm will occur. **Photo 24 - "Squeezing an elbow."**

Paragraph 5. BIE CHI: Holding by wings.

From paragraph 3 throughout paragraph 5 it is necessary to exercise with a sparring partner. Particular movements must be mastered well, then they should be executed in succession as a single technique. Only in that way skills of "pressing", "joining", "rotating", and "circling" can be developed.

As in the previous case, this technique is used if the course of executing the above method "Gripping by a shoulder" the enemy tries to slip out and free himself from a grip.

Explanations

B(A) seized A(B) by the left (right) shoulder with his right (left) hand. A(B) started to use the method ZHUA JIAN (paragraph 3, "Gripping by a shoulder") with the aim to seize the enemy but B(A) perceived his intentions in time and tries to slip out. In that case A(B) must instantly thrust his left (right) hand under an enemy's armpit to some place behind the back of the enemy. It is necessary to stretch forward the right (left) arm that squeezed the right (left) hand of the enemy before, behind his back,

Photo 25 - "Holding by wings", first phase.

above his right (left) shoulder near the neck, join the palms by placing one on another and press on the shoulder of the enemy with force. As a result of it the enemy will be forced to bend forward and his right (left) arm will be above your left (right) shoulder. You must press down with both arms and toward

- 57 -

you, raise your left (right) shoulder up, move the whole torso forward. As a consequence the enemy's head will bend toward his legs and his posture will resemble rifles in a rack. In that case it is important not to give the enemy a chance to make a somersault. If an abrupt force is applied, a dislocation of the shoulder joint will occur. **Photo 25: the first phase of the method "Holding by wings."**

Continuation

If B(A) has a supple body, the effect may not be got. In that case A(B) must bend further forward, seize the left (right) shoulder of the enemy with both hands and pull to himself, concurrently press with his left (right) shoulder forward. In that case a dislocation of the enemy's right (left) shoulder will certainly occur. If he continues pulling to himself with both arms, a dislocation of the second shoulder of the enemy will also occur. **Photo 26: the second phase of the method "Holding by wings."**

Photo 26 - "Holding by wings", second phase.

Paragraph 6. JIA BI TUO JIAN: Squeezing arms, dislocating shoulders.

This method is used if the enemy is in a lying or sitting position.

Explanations

A(B), taking advantage that B(A) sits or lies, rushes toward him from above, kneels down, squeezes him on sides with the knees and the shins and does not give him a chance to turn over. It turns out that B(A) lies on his back, as a rule in that position he tries to strike with arms or seize the attacking man by the throat. Using it, A(B) seizes the arms of the enemy with his hands crosswise (enemy's right arm with his right hand, the left arm with his left hand) and presses them to the ground beyond the enemy's head. Then A(B) leans forward and jumps over the head of the enemy with a support on his arms and a turn by 180 degrees. His arms remain at the same place, only his torso changes its position.

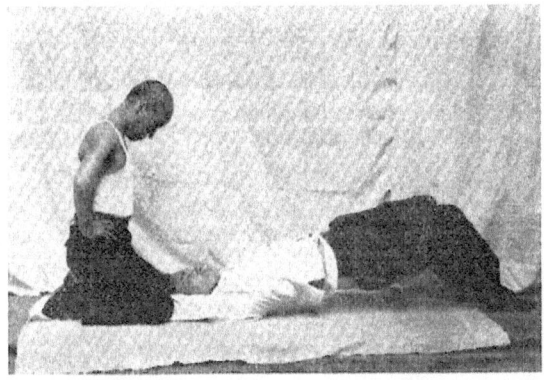

Photo 27: "Squeezing arms, dislocating shoulders."

It is necessary to squeeze upper parts of the arms of the enemy on sides with knees after landing, raise the enemy's head a little and press inward with the knees. The shoulder-blades of B(A) will converge and a dislocation of both shoulder joints will occur. **Photo 27: "Squeezing arms, dislocating shoulders."**

SHAOLIN CHIN NA

Part IV.
XIOUNG LEI BEI BU NA FA

Countermeasures against Grips from the front, flanks and the rear

Paragraph 1. HOU TUO ZHOU: Propping up an elbow from the rear.

The method of freeing oneself from a grip on the collar from the rear is almost completely identical to the above described method of freeing oneself from a grip on the hair from the rear. See part 1, paragraph 3.

This method is used if the enemy seized you by the collar from the rear.

Explanations

A(B) is going or standing, B(A) imperceptibly approaches him from behind and seizes with the right (left) hand by the collar. A(B), without turning round, covers the hand of the enemy that seized his collar with his right (left) hand and firmly squeezes it in the region of the wrist. Then it is necessary to step with the right (left) leg forward immediately, concurrently bending the upper part of the torso a little forward.

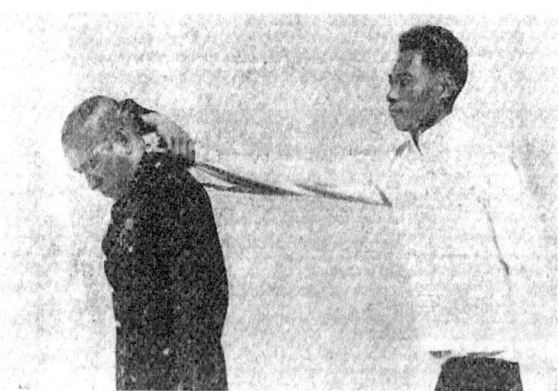

Photo 28 - "Propping up an elbow from the rear", first phase.

That is the first, preparatory, phase of the method. **Photo 28: the first phase of the method "Propping up an elbow from the rear."**

Continuation

After A(B) has seized the enemy's hand that holds him by the collar with his right (left) hand he must turn to the left (right) and get to the right flank of B(A), immediately propping up the elbow of the held arm of the enemy from below with left (right) palm and pushing it up. At the same time he must slightly squat by bending legs in knees a little bit, throw his head back, the right (left) hand that squeezes the wrist of the enemy near the collar moves together with the body. All movements must be

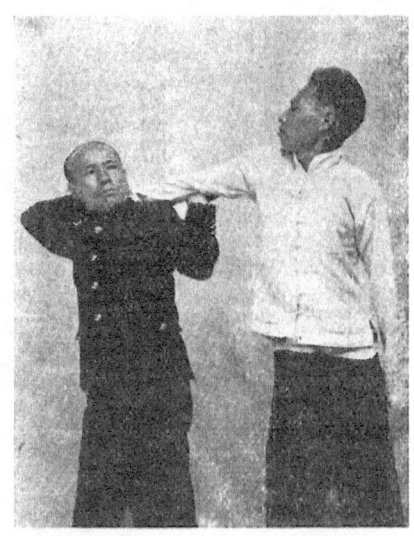

Photo 29 - "Propping up an elbow from the rear", second phase.

done fast and in a coordinated manner, in that case a fracture of the elbow joint of the enemy is inevitable. **Photo 29: the second phase of the method "Propping up an elbow from the rear."**

Paragraph 2. BO ZHOU: Pressing on an elbow.

This method is used if the enemy, as in the previous case, seized you by the collar from the rear.

Photo 30- "Pressing on an elbow."

Explanations

B(A), being behind the back of A(B), seized him by the collar with the right (left) hand. With the right hand A(B) instantly covers and firmly squeezes the hand of the enemy that holds his collar. Immediately after that A(B) steps back and aside with the right (left) leg, his torso slightly turns to the left, the left (right) arm quickly rises up and bends in elbow, then moves forward and down. It is necessary to press on the elbow of the enemy's held arm from above with the left (right) forearm. During those actions the right (left) hand must firmly hold (fix) the enemy's hand near your collar and must not allow it to slip out, the left (right) leg must be abruptly straightened to the left and backward right to the enemy's feet as if you trip him up. Here the coordination of actions is necessary: the body slightly leans forward and turns to the right (left), the left (right) leg pushes back and to the left (right). All movements must be done quickly and in a coordinated manner, never linger. **Photo 30: "Pressing on an elbow."**

Paragraph 3. ZHUANG SHEN DUAN WAN: Turning the torso and fracturing a wrist.

The correct grip of an enemy's hand is the key point for controlling over the whole arm of the enemy. If the method is executed correctly, the shape of the enemy's arm corresponds to the following sketch:

(elbow) 肘

(wrist) 腕

肩 (shoulder)

This method is used if the enemy seizes you by your collar from the front.

Explanations

A and B are going beside each other in the same direction. Suddenly B(A) stretches his right (left) arm and seizes B(A) by the collar from the front. A(B) instantly covers the hand of the enemy with his right (left) hand and thrusts his middle finger under the enemy's palm. Concurrently the left (right) arm strikes an abrupt blow from above downward at the point QU CHI that is available on the inner side of the bend of the elbow, as a result of it the arm of the

Photo 31 - "Turning the torso and fracturing a wrist."

enemy bends. It is necessary, not allowing the enemy to

straighten the arm, to swing immediately to the right (left) by 90 degrees. A fracture of the wrist will occur. **Photo 31: "Turning the torso and fracturing a wrist."**

Paragraph 4. WO TI: Lying hoof.

This method is used if the enemy seized you by the collar not too firmly. Otherwise, for a successful use of the method it is necessary to have a high level of skill or considerably surpass the enemy in force.

This method is used if the enemy seized you by the collar from the front.

Explanations

B(A) seized A(B) for the collar from the front with the right (left) hand. A(B) covers the hand of the enemy with his right (left) hand and firmly presses toward him, thrusting his middle finger under the palm of the enemy.

Photo 32 - "Lying hoof", first phase.

Simultaneously A(B) presses on the held arm of the enemy, about one CUN (3.33 cm, or 1.312 in) up the wrist, from below upward with his left (right) palm. Both elbows must be firmly pressed to the torso and drawn together. Then it is necessary to proceed to the second phase of the method as described below. **Photo 32: the first phase of the method "Lying hoof."**

Continuation

A(B) must abruptly move with the whole of his torso forward and immediately shift back. It is done to disorganize the enemy and weaken his resistance. Concurrently press on an enemy's arm near the wrist to the right (left) and down with the outer edge of the left (right) palm, i.e. from the side of the little finger, so his hand will turn with the palm up and the wrist will bend. During those actions it is necessary to turn the torso a little to the right (left) and then abruptly tilt it forward. Your forearms and elbows must be tightly pressed to the torso so that arms and torso can move as a single whole. It is necessary to use the weight of the whole body and "explosive" effort for pressing forward and downward and the enemy will have to bend down and touch the ground with his free hand. At that instant you will hear a cracking of the fractured wrist. **Photo 33: the second phase of the method "Lying hoof."**

Photo 33 - "Lying hoof", second phase.

Paragraph 5. CUI ZHOU: Fracturing an elbow.

Sometimes this method is called "A boatsman punts the boat." If the man in black clothes (see photo 34) draws his left leg back, his posture will look like it is shown here:

In that case a destructive effect from the force acting on the enemy's elbow will be substantially greater.

The method is used if the enemy seized you by the collar from the front.

Explanations

B(A), being in front of A(B), seizes him by the collar with the right (left) hand. A(B) instantly covers the hand of B(A) with his right (left) hand and firmly squeezes it. At that moment A(B) makes a push with his breast forward and the enemy instinctively tries to push him away. At once A(B) follows the direction of force applied by the enemy and moves a little back, as a

Photo 34 - "Fracturing an elbow."

result of it the right (left) arm of the enemy unbends in elbow. At that moment A(B) abruptly turns to the right (left) by 90 degrees, at that his left (right) arm rises up and strikes a blow with the forearm at the enemy's elbow from above downward.

At the moment of striking a blow at the elbow it is necessary to turn the upper part of the torso a little to the right (left) and slightly tilt it forward. If the enemy resists, a more radical variant can be chosen: to put the left leg back, right by the feet of the enemy, exactly as in the method BO ZHOU (see section 4, paragraph 2 "Pressing on an elbow"). In that case the elbow will be certainly damaged. **Photo 34: "Fracturing an elbow."**

Paragraph 6. DING WAN: Propping a wrist.

It is a good method but one must act very fast. One who wears the black clothes must bend a little forward. Schematically the arm of the enemy must look so:

The method is used if the enemy tries to seize you by the chest.

Explanations

B(A) stretches the right (left) arm, he is going to seize A(B) by the clothes on the left side of the chest. When the hand of B(A) is at the point of seizing A(B) but has not seized yet (please pay attention to it – that is a key moment) A(B) seizes the enemy by the arm a little up the elbow with his left (right) hand.

Concurrently he delivers an energetic blow from above on the wrist of B(A) with the edge of his right (left) palm, owing to it the wrist bends, the hand turns with the palm up and the back side of the palm props against the left (right) side of the chest of A(B). At that instant the right (left) hand of A(B) seizes the arm of the enemy a little up the elbow above his own left hand. You must pull to you with both arms, tilt the upper part of torso and stick out the breast forward. It is necessary to press with force so the enemy will not be able to unbend the wrist. **Photo 35: "Propping a wrist."**

Photo 35 - "Propping a wrist."

Paragraph 7. JIE WAN: Picking up a wrist.

Here requirements to the execution of the method are similar to those ones described in the previous paragraph. Schematically the arm of the enemy must look so:

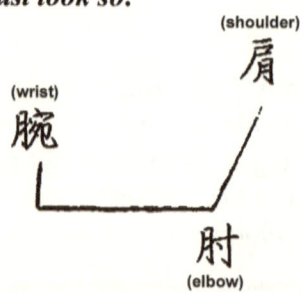

The method is used if the enemy, as in the previous case, tries to seize you by your clothes on the breast.

Explanations

B(A) approaches A(B) from the front and stretches his right (left) arm with the palm down, intending to seize A(B) by the clothes on the breast. When B(A) is on the verge of seizing, A(B) draws in his breast and shifts a little back, concurrently seizing the right (left) arm of B(A) a little up the elbow with his left (right) hand. At that time the right (left) arm of A(B) strikes from below at the right (left) wrist of B(A), that causes the wrist to bend

Photo 36 - "Picking up a wrist."

down and prop against the breast of A(B). The blow must be delivered with the edge of the palm on the side of the thumb, the four fingers must be straightened and closely pressed to each other, the thumb must stick aside. Following that, A(B) immediately and firmly seizes the right (left) hand of B(A) with his right (left) hand and pulls toward him with force, concurrently sticking out his breast. It is of no importance if the held arm is bent in elbow or not. The most important thing is to firmly fix the wrist to prevent the enemy from moving it up, down, or to sides. **Photo 36: "Picking up a wrist."**

Paragraph 8. FAN TUO ZHOU: Propping an elbow inward.

At the initial stage (of this method) actions are completely similar to those ones described in paragraph 3 of this section and shown in photo 31. The only difference is that in this case the location of seizing is further up.

This method is used if the enemy seized you by your clothes on the breast, near the neck, right under your chin.

Explanations

B(A) approaches A(B) from the front and seizes him by the clothes on the breast, near the neck, right under the chin. A(B) must instantly cover the hand of the enemy with the right (left) hand and concurrently deliver a "chopping" blow from above downward at the inner side of the elbow bend of the caught arm of the enemy in the region of the point QU CHI with the left (right) hand. Due to those actions the arm of the enemy bends and his torso tilts forward.

Photo 37 - "Propping an elbow inward."

At that moment A(B) starts pressing on the enemy's elbow from the left to the right (from the right to the left) with the left (right) palm, concurrently turning to the right (left) on the left (right) foot. After turning to the enemy sideways, i.e. by 90 degrees, it is necessary to tilt the upper part of the torso a little back and make an energetic upward push from below with the left (right) palm. A fracture of the elbow will occur. **Photo 37: "Propping an elbow inward."**

SHAOLIN CHIN NA

Part V.
YAO FU BU NA FA
Counteractions against Grips on the Waist and Stomach

Paragraph 1. QIAN PENG ZHOU: Pressing on an elbow from the front.

As to technique this method is similar to the method CUI ZHOU – "Fracturing an elbow" (See section 4, paragraph 5, photo 34). The only difference is that in this case the location of seizing is lower.

This method is used if the enemy seized you by your waist belt or clothes in the region of your waist.

Explanations

B(A) seizes A(B) by the belt or clothes on the waist with the left (right) hand, his arm with the palm down. With the left (right) palm A(B) instantly covers the hand of the enemy which has caught him by the belt or clothes in the region of the waist, firmly squeezes and presses it toward himself and does not allow the enemy to remove the arm. Simultaneously it is necessary to make a pull toward yourself with force, using the whole body, so the arm of the enemy unbends in elbow and then

Photo 38 - "Pressing on the elbow from the front."

immediately make a big step forward with the right (left) leg, right by the enemy's feet so that your calf muscle props against the shin of the enemy. It is necessary to tilt low forward in that position, the arm of the enemy caught by you being under your right (left) armpit and its forearm being pressed to your chest ribs. One must press down and forward on the elbow of the enemy with the right (left) elbow, concurrently turning the upper part of the torso a little to the left (right). All those movements must be executed very fast, otherwise it will not work. **Photo 38: "Pressing on the elbow from the front."**

Paragraph 2. HOU PENG ZHOU: Pressing on an elbow from the rear.

This method is used if the enemy, being behind your back, seized you by the waist belt or clothes in the region of the waist.

Explanations

A(B) is going or standing, B(A) approaches from the rear and seizes him by the belt or clothes in the region of the waist. A(B) instantly moves the right (left) arm behind the back and firmly catches the hand of the enemy. Immediately after that A(B) takes a stride forward with the right (left) leg and pulls the enemy after him with force. It is the first phase of the method **"Pressing on an elbow from the rear"**, see photo 39.

Photo 39 - "Pressing on an elbow from the rear", first phase.

Continuation

A(B) turns with his left (right) side to the enemy, raises left (right) arm, draws it back and lowers it behind the held enemy's arm, closes fingers to each other and thrusts the palm under the armpit of the enemy from the side of the enemy's back toward the enemy's breast, as a result of it the back side of the left (right) palm of A(B) is pressed to the enemy's breast. At that moment A(B) moves his left (right) leg to the left (right) to be placed in front of the right (left) leg of the enemy and tilts his torso forward. In that position the left (right) arm presses on the elbow of the enemy from above down, the head and the upper part of the torso being turned a little to the right and back as if you wish to turn round. The right (left) arm also pulls to the right and back with force. **Photo 40: the second phase of the method "Pressing on an elbow from the rear."**

Photo 40 - "Pressing on an elbow from the rear", second phase.

Paragraph 3. DING WAN: Propping a wrist.

This method is used if the enemy seized you by the waist belt or clothes in the region of the stomach from the front.

Explanations

B(A) approaches A(B) from the front and seizes by the belt with the right (left) hand. A(B) strains DAN TIAN and sticks out the lower part of the stomach, concurrently moving with the whole body a little forward and immediately backward. At that moment A(B) seizes the right (left) arm of the enemy a little up the elbow with the left (right) hand and immediately moves forward. Such movements disorganize the enemy and weaken his grip. A(B) delivers an energetic blow with the right (left) arm from above

Photo 41 - "Propping a wrist", first phase.

downward and a little aside at the wrist of the enemy, it results in bending the wrist of the right (left) arm of B(A). **It is the first phase of the method "Propping a wrist", see photo 41.**

Continuation

After the blow the wrist of B(A) has bent, the back side of his hand is pressed to the stomach of A(B). Immediately the right (left) hand of A(B) seizes the arm of the enemy a little up the elbow and pulls to it, supplementing actions of the left arm. Simultaneously A(B) sticks out the lower part of the stomach and presses forward. The movements must be strong and coordinated. It is of no importance if the arm of the enemy is bent in elbow joint or not: he feels a severe pain in his wrist and loses his ability to resist. **Photo 42: the second phase of the method "Propping a wrist".**

Photo 42 - "Propping a wrist", second phase.

Paragraph 4. DUAN ZHOU: Raising an elbow.

This method is used if the enemy seized you by the waist belt, his hand with the palm up.

Explanations

B(A) seized A(B) by the belt with the right (left) hand with the palm up. A(B) immediately tilts the upper part of the torso forward and draws back his stomach and pelvis, concurrently he seizes an arm of the enemy with both hands a little up the elbow and pulls to himself with force and presses downward with the breast. As a consequence of those actions the enemy bends forward. At that moment A(B) sets his left (right) foot against the right

Photo 43 - "Raising an elbow."

(left) hip joint of the enemy and presses forward and down with force, while carrying on to pull to him with both arms, and shifts the upper part of the torso back. Movements of torso, arms and leg must be coordinated, fast and strong. A fracture of the elbow joint will occur. **Photo 43: "Raising an elbow."**

Paragraph 5. KUA ZHOU: Linking your arm through enemy's arm.

During the execution of this method force must be applied with a jerk, you must act fast and unexpectedly for the enemy, in that case you can fracture his elbow. It is dangerous to be slow.

This method is used if the enemy seized you by your waist belt, his hand with the palm up.

Explanations

B(A) seized A(B) by the waist belt, at that the hand of B(A) is with the palm up. With his right (left) hand A(B) instantly seizes the hand of the enemy which has caught him by the belt and firmly holds it, not allowing to get free. Concurrently it is necessary to tilt the upper part of the body forward, move back your stomach and pull toward you with force as to straighten the held arm of the enemy. At that moment you as if link your arm through the enemy's arm: you press on his arm at a place a

Photo 44 - "Linking your arm through enemy's arm."

little up the elbow upward from below with the inner side of the elbow bend. At that your right (left) arm presses down, the upper part of the body leans back, due to it the enemy is forced to stand on tiptoe, then a fracture of the elbow joint will occur. **Photo 44: "Linking your arm through enemy's arm."**

Paragraph 6. LE WAN: Pressing on a wrist.

This method is used if the enemy seized you by the waist belt, the hand is with the palm up.

Explanations

B(A) with his palm up is going to seize A(B) by the waist belt or the clothes in the region of the stomach. At the moment when the enemy has already stretched his arm and is at the verge of seizing you must seize the enemy by an arm in the region of the elbow with your left (right) hand and pull toward you. Concurrently you must close up and straighten fingers on the right (left) palm, strike at the wrist of the enemy with the edge of the palm from above down so that the wrist is bent and pressed to your

Photo 45 - " Pressing on a wrist."

stomach. Immediately you stick out your stomach, seize the arm of the enemy above your left (right) hand with the right (left) hand and pull with both arms toward you and down, concurrently pushing forward the lower part of the stomach. A fracture of the wrist will occur. **Photo 45: "Pressing on a wrist."**

Paragraph 7. DUAN YAO: Fracturing the waist.

A possibility to carry out this method exists far from always, one must have a good level of training and sufficient experience. Otherwise you will fail.

This method is not independent one, a chance to use it must be prepared through previous actions, otherwise it is difficult to succeed. We kindly ask those who exercise to pay attention to this fact.

Explanations

A(B), carrying out some actions, knocks B(A) down. If the enemy falls down on the right of you, it is necessary to put the right thigh under in order him to fall on it with his waist, if on the left of you – the left thigh, taking at that the stance of Unicorn (QI LIN). At the same time you place your left (right) hand on the enemy's chest and the right (left) hand on his pubis bone. If you abruptly press down with both arms and raise the left (right) leg a little up, the enemy's spine will fracture. **Photo 46: "Fracturing the waist."**

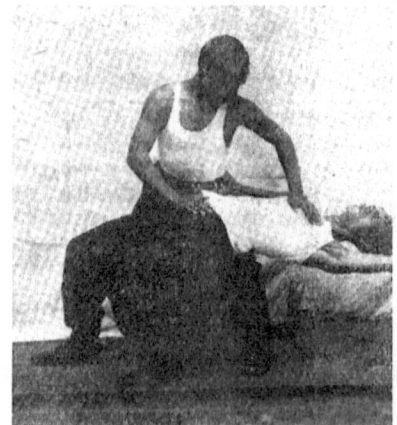

Photo 46 - "Fracturing the waist."

Paragraph 8. JIA YAO: Squeezing the waist.

It is necessary to have sufficient strength and have a good level of skill for a successful use of this method. Untrained people will hardly be able to do it.

This is a case when a man, as it seems, is in a losing position, uses it to his advantage and wins. If the enemy furiously rushes at you and you have no time to dodge, you feint falling down on the ground.

Explanations

B(A) rapidly attacks A(B). A(B) realizes that he has no time to dodge the attack and falls down his back carrying the enemy with him and raising his legs to clasp the waist of the enemy. After falling on the back it is necessary to cross your legs behind the back of the enemy immediately and to squeeze his body from sides as strong as possible with your thighs and knees, that will lead to a fracture of ribs and damage of the diaphragm. If your legs are short and the waist of the enemy is thick, this method is unacceptable. One should not thoughtlessly use this method, as it will be impossible to save the man in case of a serious damage of the diaphragm. **Photo 47: "Squeezing the waist."**

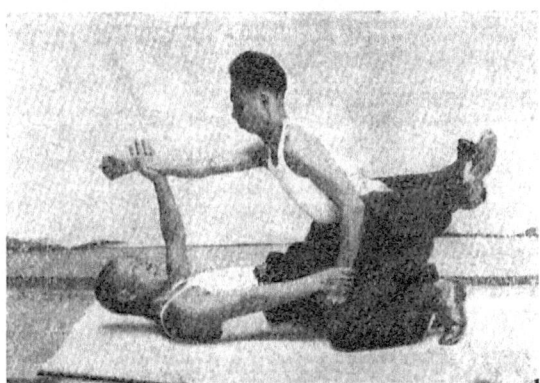

Photo 47 - "Squeezing the waist."

擒拿法

SHAOLIN CHIN NA

Part VI.
BI WAN BU NA FA
Grips on the Arm and
Wrist

Paragraph 1. XIAO CHAN SI: Small hank of thread.

When a bobbin rotates, thread can be wound on it. That is the gist of the method. Two types of arm movements can be distinguished in this method: shuttle movement and spiral-type wrist movement.

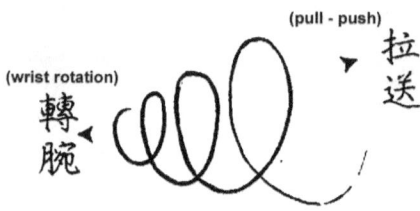

This method is used if the enemy seized you by a wrist.

Explanations

A(B) intends to seize B(A) with the right (left) hand; however, as soon as he stretched his arm the enemy seized him by the wrist. In that case A(B) must immediately cover the hand of the enemy that squeezes his wrist with the left (right) hand and firmly seize it, not allowing the enemy to free himself. At that the thumb of the left (right) hand of A(B) is below and the other four fingers above. Further shuttle movement is made with the following purpose: if you, for instance, make a push from yourself and the enemy applies force in the opposite direction, you suddenly start pulling toward you and the force of the enemy can be directed against himself. For that purpose it is necessary to make an abrupt push forward with arms and immediately pull toward you, moving arms up and back to straighten the enemy's arm in elbow and bend the enemy's wrist down. **It is the first phase of the method "Small hank of thread", see photo 48.**

Photo 48 - "Small hank of thread", first phase.

Continuation

A(B) pulls up and back (toward himself), owing to it the held arm of the enemy straightens in elbow and its wrist bends. At that moment A(B) must seize the arm of the enemy in a place one CUN (3.33 cm, or 1.312 in) up the wrist with the right (left) hand from above, the thumb rings round the forearm from one side and the other fingers from the other side. At that, it is necessary to press to the left

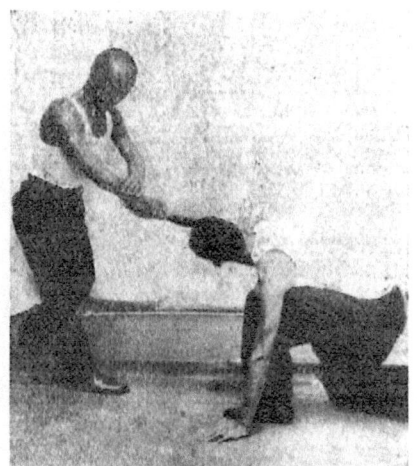

Photo 49 - "Small hank of thread", second phase.

(right) and down with the tip of the middle finger to bend the wrist of the enemy aside so that he can not turn it. A(B) must press down and pull toward him with the arms and the enemy will be forced to kneel on one knee and touch the ground with his free hand. In that position he feels violent pain in the wrist and loses his ability to resist. If necessary, make a strong pull to you and down, a fracture of the wrist will occur. It is the second phase of the method **"Small hank of thread", see photo 49.**

Paragraph 2. SHUANG CHAN SI: Double hank of thread.

This method is used as a countermeasure against the above-described method, i.e. when the enemy uses a counter-grip "Small hank of thread" against your grip.

Explanations

A(B) seized the arm of B(A) by the wrist, but B(A) immediately proceeded to the method "Small hank of thread" and covered the hand of A(B) with his palm. At that moment when B(A) did not apply maximum effort yet, A(B) must neutralize the force applied by the enemy to his wrist. To do that, you should raise the right (left) elbow up to the level of the shoulder or higher and raise the left (right) arm with the palm toward you vertically in

Photo 50 - "Double hank of thread", first phase.

front of the breast between the arms of the enemy. It is necessary raise your caught arm and both arms of the enemy with the upper part of the left (right) arm so that you do not feel pain in the wrist of the caught arm. **It is the first phase of the method "Double hank of thread", see photo 50.**

Continuation

A(B) covers the right (left) hand of the enemy with his left (right) hand, firmly seizes the middle finger or all fingers of B(A) and pulls down and toward him with force, the left (right) hand of A(B) being turned with the palm inward. At the same time the right (left) arm of A(B) also presses down, its elbow must be kept at the level of the hand (the forearm is in the horizontal position). Both arms must be firmly pressed to the breast of A(B) and must not pulled off the breast at any event.

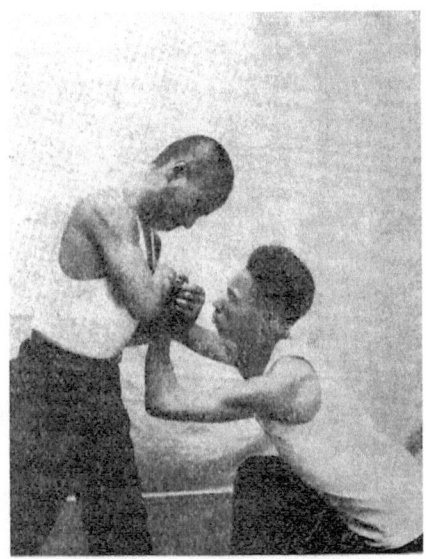

Photo 51 - "Double hank of thread", second phase.

Then it is necessary to stand tiptoe, step forward, tilt the upper part of the body a little forward and bend knees a little, concurrently and strongly pressing down with both arms. In that case the enemy will be forced to kneel down and lose his ability to resist. If you press with the left (right) arm strong enough, the right (left) arm can be pulled off and one arm can hold both arms of the enemy. **Photo 51: the second phase of the method "Double hank of thread."**

Paragraph 3. DA CHAN SI: Big hank of thread.

This method is essentially similar to the method "Small hank of thread", but it allows to apply greater force. Even if the enemy is strong, his strength is compensated by lateral force of your elbow.

This method is used when you encounter a physically strong enemy and the method XIAO CHAN SI ("Small hank of thread", paragraph 1) can be ineffective against him.

Photo 52 - "Big hank of thread", first phase.

Explanations

A(B) stretched the right (left) arm with the intention to seize B(A), but B(A) immediately seized A(B) by a wrist with his right (left) hand. A(B) sizes the opportunity and pulls the right (left) arm toward himself, at the same time he makes a step forward with the left (right) leg and puts his foot on the ground in front of the right (left) foot of the enemy, a little closer to the central line. While doing those actions, A(B) becomes turned to the enemy with his left (right) side. At that moment A(B) bends the left (right) arm and presses upward from below on the caught arm of the enemy with the inner side of the elbow bend. **It is the first phase of the method "Big hank of thread", photo 52.**

Photo 53 - "Big hank of thread", second phase.

The second phase of the method "Big hank of thread"

A(B), carrying on the method, raises up the bent left (right) arm and simultaneously pulls to the right (left) and downward with the right (left) arm without giving the enemy the chance to free himself. Then A(B) covers from above the right (left) hand of the enemy with the left (right) hand and pulls toward himself with force with both arms. **It is the second phase of the method "Big hank of thread", photo 53.**

The third phase of the method "Big hank of thread"

Continuation. The force of the right (left) arm of A(B) is directed to him and downward, concurrently he presses down with the left (right) forearm, however, the forearm must be kept horizontally. The body tilts a little forward and to the left as if you are going to turn back. As a result of those actions B(A) will certainly kneel down. If great force is applied, a fracture of the wrist may occur, the enemy has no any chance to resist. **It is the third phase of the method "Big hank of thread", photo 54.**

Photo 54 - "Big hank of thread", third phase.

Paragraph 4. QU ZHOU DUAN BI: Bending an elbow and fracturing an arm.

Having mastered the method "Big hank of thread" well, it will be easier to acquire this method. Here the key to success also lies in elbow work and a lateral force.

Method is used when the enemy delivers an arm blow downward from above.

Explanations

A(B) and B(A) go in the same direction beside each other or they go toward each other – in both cases actions of A(B) will be the same. B(A) suddenly attacks, striking down from above at the head, the collar-bone or the neck of A(B). A(B) wards off the blow of

Photo 55 - "Bending an elbow and fracturing an arm", first phase.

the enemy with the left (right) forearm and simultaneously

- 92 -

moves his left (right) leg forward. **It is the first phase of the method "Bending an elbow and fracturing an arm", photo 55.**

The second phase of the method "Bending an elbow and fracturing an arm"

A(B) makes a step forward with the right (left) leg, bends the right (left) arm in elbow and raises it on the outer side of the enemy's arm, then he makes a strong jerk to the right (left) and toward himself. Simultaneously A(B) pushes away with the forearm of the left (right) arm, his left (right) fist opens into the palm which seizes the wrist of the right (left) arm of the enemy. As a result the right (left) arm of the enemy becomes bent in elbow and can not slip off the grip. **It is the second phase of the method "Bending an elbow and fracturing an arm", photo 56.**

Photo 56 - "Bending an elbow and fracturing an arm", second phase.

- 93 -

The third phase of the method "Bending an elbow and fracturing an arm"

Finding himself in such a position, B(A) will certainly try to free himself or somehow counterattack. But whatever actions B(A) will try to carry out, A(B) must instantly lower his right (left) hand and seize the right (left) arm of the enemy three CUNs (9.99 cm, or 3.93 in) up the wrist with three fingers – the middle finger, the fourth finger and the little finger. It is necessary to press down with hands with force, concurrently raising up the right (left) elbow, due to it the enemy will feel violent pain in the elbow joint and

Photo 57 - "Bending an elbow and fracturing an arm", third phase.

lose his ability to resist. If the pressure is increased, a dislocation of the elbow joint will occur. **It is the third phase of the method "Bending an elbow and fracturing an arm", photo 57.**

Paragraph 5. KUA LAN: Carrying a basket by grappling it with an arm.

To use successfully this method, the key point is proper location of the point QU CHI on the elbow bend of the enemy, only then his elbow will be bent.

This method is used if the enemy tries to seize you by your clothes in the region of the breast or for locking the arm of the enemy when he is arrested.

Explanations

B(A) tries to seize A(B) for the clothes with his right (left) hand. At the very last moment when B(A) has already stretched out his arm and is at the point of seizing, left (right) hand of A(B) with the palm up must seize B(A) by the hand with a

Photo 58 - "Carrying a basket by grappling it with an arm", first phase.

quick movement. Concurrently A(B) seizes the right (left) arm of the enemy in the region of the elbow bend with his right (left) hand, the thumb grapples from above and four other fingers from below. At that it is necessary to press on the point QU CHI with the "Tiger's jaws" (HU KOU)[23] and vigorously push to the left (right) with the whole of the arm. **It is the first phase of the method "Carrying a basket by grappling it with an arm", photo 58.**

Editor's notes:
[23] HU KOU: lit. "tiger's jaws", space between the thumb and the forefinger.

The second phase

When A(B) using force presses the arm of the enemy in the region of the point QU CHI with the right (left) hand, the elbow of the enemy will certainly bend. At that moment A(B) bends his left (right) arm and presses with the right (left) arm to the left (right) and downward as for the right (left) arm of the enemy to be under the left (right) armpit of A(B). At that moment A(B) puts his left (right) arm round the arm of the enemy and strongly presses it toward his side, the wrist of the enemy

Photo 59 - "Carrying a basket by grappling it with an arm", second phase.

being bent and fixed. In that position the more A(B) bends his arm the more the wrist of the enemy bends. If both opponents are of approximately equal strength, in such a position B(A) completely loses his ability to resist. But if the enemy is very strong or his wrist is very supple, it is necessary, while pressing strongly with the left (right) arm as before, to thrust the thumb of the right (left) hand under the right (left) palm of the enemy and place four other fingers on the back of the palm. You must turn with the right (left) hand outward (from yourself) and inward (toward yourself) with the left (right) hand. In that case the enemy will not be able to resist and be forced to obey your orders. If the enemy should be escorted, it will be easy to do: small effort will be enough to inflict violent pain in his wrist, that will make him obey. However, if strong force is applied, a fracture of the wrist will occur. **It is the second phase of the method "Carrying a basket by grappling it with an arm", photo 59.**

Paragraph 6 FU HU: Binding a tiger.

This method is used when a criminal is arrested. To execute it, a hand of the enemy must be caught.

Explanations

A(B) and B(A) go toward each other. If B(A) has to be arrested, A(B) must move a little to the left (right) and suddenly seize the right (left) hand of B(A) with the right (left) hand, the palm turned backward. At that the thumb of A(B) is placed on the back of the hand of the enemy and four other fingers press themselves to the inner side of the hand right under the wrist. At the same moment you must strongly squeeze the hand of the enemy and pull toward yourself, the

Photo 60 - "Binding a tiger", first phase.

whole of the body shifting a little back. **It is the first phase of the method "Binding a tiger", photo 60.**

The second phase

To continue the previous action, A(B) raises his right (left) arm up and to the right (left) as for the caught arm of the enemy to be turned with the palm up. Then A(B) sets against the back of the enemy's hand with his thumbs and squeezes the enemy's palm with the other fingers near the wrist. With eight fingers A(B) presses on the enemy's wrist toward himself and down, with thumbs presses from himself, shifts the whole of his body a little back. Then A(B) immediately presses with the arms down to force the enemy to tilt forward and lean the left (right) hand against the ground, his right (left) knee is about to touch the ground. All movements must be done fast and smoothly. **It is the second phase of the method "Binding a tiger", photo 61.**

Photo 61 - "Binding a tiger", second phase.

The third phase

A(B) makes a strong and abrupt push forward and down to the ground, at the same time he takes a big step forward with the left (right) leg and lowers his foot close to the right (left) knee of B(A). In this position the upper part of the right (left) arm of B(A), his shoulder and cheek cling close to the ground, his right (left) leg is on the knee, the left leg as if is slightly raised, the left (right) arm sets against the ground. The right (left) arm of B(A) is bent up, his forearm is vertical, the palm faces the ground. A(B) must stand, greatly tilting forward, at that he must set his left (right) knee against a buttock of the enemy to prevent his somersault. **It is the third phase of the method "Binding a tiger", photo 62.**

Photo 62 - "Binding a tiger", third phase.

The fourth phase

A(B) slightly turns to the left (right), his left (right) knee sets against the right (left) buttock of the enemy with force as before, his right leg steps forward and treads on the upper part of the right (left) arm of the enemy near the shoulder. The left (right) knee of A(B) continues to press on the waist of B(A) from the side of the back and his right (left) shin pushes the right (left) forearm of the enemy forward. In this position A(B) can free

Photo 63 - "Binding a tiger", fourth phase.

his hands. It is necessary to press strongly with both legs so that the enemy will not be able to move both arms and legs. In this position the hands of A(B) are absolutely free. If he has no cord with him, he can pull of the belt of B(A) and bind him. If necessary A(B) can make a strong push with the right (left) leg forward, which will lead to dislocation of shoulder and elbow joints of the enemy. **It is the fourth phase of the method "Binding a tiger", photo 63.**

Paragraph 7. GUN ZHOU: Somersault over the elbow.

This method is quite tough, but its efficiency is significantly lower without somersault, additionally there is a risk that the enemy will manage to free himself.

This method is used when the enemy delivers a straight punch.

Explanations

B(A) attacks A(B) with a straight right (left) punch. A(B) moves a little bit back and slightly turns the upper part of the torso to the right (left) for the punch to hit "void". At the same moment A(B) strongly clasps the fist of the enemy with his left (right)

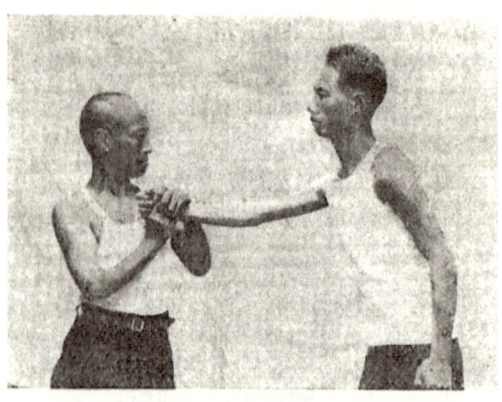

Photo 64 - "Somersault over the elbow", first phase.

hand from above and with his right (left) hand from below and pulls the fist toward him and to the right. B(A) tries to jerk his arm back and pulls it back to him. **It is the first phase of the method "Somersault over the elbow", photo 64.**

The second phase

At the instant when B(A) starts pulling his caught arm to him A(B) follows him and makes a push forward with both arms, his right (left) leg takes a big step forward and to the left (right) in the transverse direction and turns out on the right (left) of the enemy's right (left) leg, as a consequence A(B)

Photo 65 - "Somersault over the elbow", second phase.

turns with his back to the enemy. In the coarse of those actions A(B) brings his right (left) elbow over the right (left) arm of the enemy and presses the arm of the enemy to his side under the armpit with it. A(B) twists the wrist of the enemy anti-clockwise with both hands and presses forward and down with the arms. As a consequence of it the right (left) of B(A) is in a unnaturally bent position, which makes him stoop the upper part of the torso forward and to the right. In that position B(A) is deprived of the possibility to resist. **It is the second phase of the method "Somersault over the elbow", photo 65.**

The third phase

Continuing the previous actions, A(B) bends down his head, presses his chin to the breast, stoops forward and down and makes a somersault over the right (left) shoulder, bringing his whole weight on the elbow joint of the enemy. If the method was executed properly, a fracture of the enemy's elbow joint will occur. It is possible to exercise only the first and the second phases of the method during training sessions without proceeding to the third one, otherwise serious body damages can occur. **It is the third phase of the method "Somersault over the elbow", photo 66.**

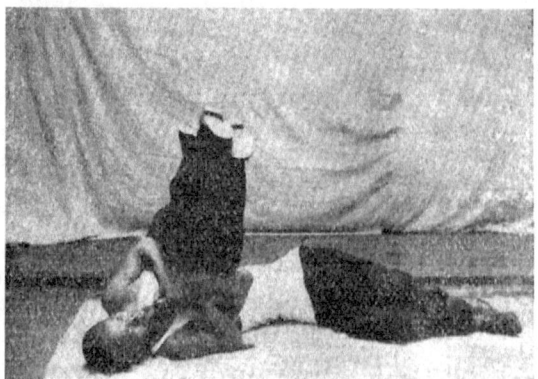

Photo 66 - "Somersault over the elbow", third phase.

Paragraph 8. CHE CHI: Pulling by the wing.

The key point here is an impact on the wrist of the enemy and a correct grip of his palm.

This method is used if the enemy tries to seize you by your clothes in the region of the breast.

Explanations

B(A) approaching from the front or a side intends to seize A(B) by the clothes in the region of the breast with his right (left) hand. At the last moment when B(A) has already stretched his arm and is about to seize, A(B) must quickly catch the stretched palm of the enemy with his left (right) hand with the palm turned outside. Simultaneously A(B) hooks the wrist of the caught arm of the enemy with the right (left) hooked wrist and makes a vigorous jerk back (toward himself) so that the wrist of the enemy will be bent and raised a little. After that it is necessary to proceed to the below-described actions at once, otherwise you yourself will be seized by the enemy. **It is the first phase of the method "Pulling by the wing", photo 67**.

Photo 67 - "Pulling by the wing", first phase.

The second phase

Continuing the above-described actions, A(B) rotates the caught palm of the enemy to the left (right) with the left (right) hand and presses down. Simultaneously with the right (left) hand A(B) seizes the palm of the enemy from the side of its thumb, sets his thumb against the back of the enemy's palm and clasps with the other four fingers from the side of the palm. Then A(B) pulls toward him with both arms and presses down, shifting his whole body a little back. As a consequence B(A) is forced to stoop forward with his right (left) side, his right (left) arm being bent in elbow and wrist. If A(B) applies a vigorous effort, a fracture of the enemy's arm will occur. **It is the second phase of the method "Pulling by the wing", photo 68.**

Photo 68 - "Pulling by the wing", second phase.

Paragraph 9. SI CHI: Tearing the wing.

This method is used for a sudden arrest of the enemy who is going toward you.

Explanations

A(B) sees B(A) whom he must arrest go toward him. After coming up to B(A) A(B) takes a step to the left (right) to be near the right (left) side of the enemy. At that moment A(B) turns his right (left) hand with the palm outside and seizes the right (left) hand of the enemy so that his thumb sets against the back of the enemy's hand and four other fingers clasp the hand from the inner side near the wrist. The grip must be strong. **It is the first phase of the method "Tearing the wing", photo 69.**

Photo 69 - "Tearing the wing", first phase.

The second phase

Continuing the previous actions, A(B) raises the caught arm of the enemy to the right (left) and upward with the right (left) arm. At that A(B) presses on the back of the hand of the enemy outward (from himself) with the thumb of the right hand and inward (to himself) with the other four fingers so that the wrist will be bent up.

Immediately the left (right) hand of A(B) comes to help the right (left) hand and seizes the hand of the enemy in a similar way: the thumb outside and the other fingers inside. A(B) with his whole body moves back, twists with both hands to the right (clockwise) with force and pulls back. Due to it B(A) is forced to stoop forward, he feels pain in the wrist and loses his ability to resist. If A(B) makes a strong jerk, a fracture of the wrist will occur. **It is the second phase of the method "Tearing the wing", photo 70.**

Photo 70 - "Tearing the wing", second phase.

The third phase

If B(A) is an experienced opponent and he is supple enough, he will try to slip out from the grip. For that B(A) has to approach A(B), bend the elbow of his right (left) arm and turn with the upper torso to the left and backward to try to catch A(B) with his left (right) hand and squeeze his throat. Having a certain skill, B(A) can succeed, therefore A(B) must not be slow in that situation. As soon as B(A) starts turning, A(B) with the right (left) arm

Photo 71 - "Tearing the wing", third phase.

must make a strong pull of the held arm of the enemy up along the enemy's back, seize the right or left shoulder of the enemy with the left (right) hand and press down with force. Those actions will force the enemy to stop his maneuver and deprive him of the ability to resist. If A(B) energetically applies force, a dislocation of the shoulder joint of B(A) will occur. **It is the third phase of the method "Tearing the wing", photo 71.**

Paragraph 10. KANG ZHOU: Carrying an elbow on the shoulder.

When you use this method, you should take into account the difference in stature.

This method is used when the enemy approaches from the front and delivers a straight blow at your head.

Explanations

B(A) approaches A(B) from the front and delivers a straight punch with the right (left) fist. A(B) slightly moves his head to the left (right) and concurrently clasps the enemy's fist with the right (left) hand from above and the left (right) hand from below, fingers of both hands of A(B) being turned to the right (left). At the same moment A(B) pulls the caught arm of the enemy toward himself, simultaneously turns back over the right (left) shoulder to 180 degrees so that

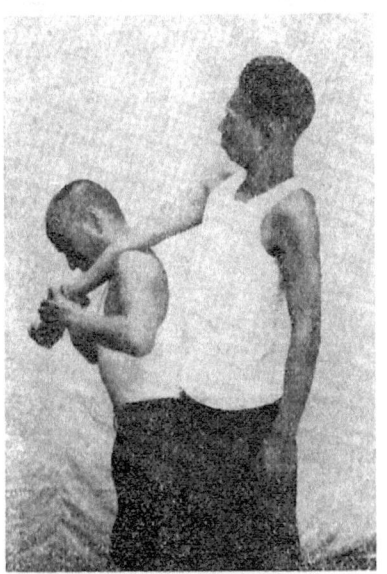

Photo 72 - "Carrying an elbow on the shoulder.

the right (left) arm of the enemy turns out lying on the left (right) shoulder of A (B). A(B) pulls the held arm of B(A) down

- 107 -

with both arms and pushes up with the shoulder, at that the body of A(B) moves a little bit forward. As a consequence B(A) has to straighten his back and tiptoe, at that he completely loses his ability to resist. If A(B) applies an energetic effort, a fracture of the elbow joint of the enemy will occur. **Photo 72 – "Carrying an elbow on the shoulder."**

Paragraph 11. JUAN QUAN: Wringing a fist.

The gist of this method lies in quickness of response and coordination of actions.

This method is used when the enemy approaches you from the front and punches from below upward.

Explanations

B(A) approaches A(B) from the front and punches at the enemy's stomach from below upward with his right (left) fist[24]. A(B) must instantly move the torso to the left (right) and squeeze the fist of the enemy with both hands, the thumbs of A(B) must be on the back side of the fist and eight other fingers squeeze the inner side of the enemy's wrist. A(B) rotates the fist of the enemy to the left (right) side, trying to turn it to 180 degrees. Simultaneously A(B) presses down with the hands and moves back with the whole body, all the actions must be done fast and with force. As a consequence B(A) will fall on his knees and the wrist of his right (left) arm will be broken. **Photo 73 – "Wringing a fist."**

Editor's notes:
[24] This blow corresponds to the uppercut in the British boxing.

Photo 73 - "Wringing a fist."

Paragraph 12. LUO WAN: Clutching a wrist.

Here is the matter not only in skill and force: it is necessary to know exactly the location of acupuncture points.

The gist of this method is an impact on acupuncture points which cause numbing. They are twin points located a little up the elbow, on the lateral surfaces of the arm, one CUN (3.33 cm, or 1.312 in) from the point QU CHI. The method is used if a criminal must be detained.

Explanations

A(B) seizes the left hand of B(A) with the left (right) hand. You must seize firmly, at that your thumb must be on the side of enemy's palm, the other fingers must clasp the back side of the enemy's hand. A(B) presses concurrently with the thumb and the middle finger of the right (left) hand on the upper and lower "points of numbing" on the left (right) arm of the enemy respectively. It is necessary to press as strong as possible and pull toward yourself so that the enemy will feel numbing and weakness in the whole body. **It is the first phase of the method "Clutching a wrist", photo 74.**

Photo 74 - "Clutching a wrist", first phase.

The second phase

B(A) will certainly try to jerk back the arm, he will try to raise the elbow up and free himself. A(B) immediately uses it for his purposes: he makes a strong push forward and up with his left (right) arm to bend the enemy's arm in elbow and then pulls toward himself to bend down the wrist of the enemy. At the same time A(B) pushes the enemy's elbow from himself with the right (left) arm. It is necessary to act fast and with force, in that case a fracture of the enemy's wrist will occur. **It is the second phase of the method "Clutching a wrist", photo 75.**

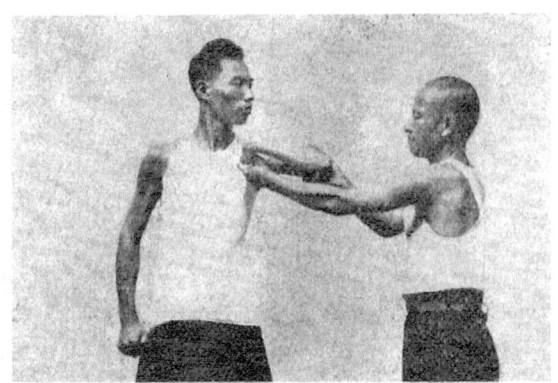

Photo 75 - "Clutching a wrist", second phase.

Paragraph 13. JIA SHAN: Squeezing with the armpit.

Here the most important thing is quickness of response and skilful movements, the stature and strength of the enemy are of no great significance at that.

This method is used when the enemy attacks you with a straight punch from the front in the region of the breast.

Explanations

B(A) resolutely attacks and punches with the left (right) fist in the region of the breast of A(B). A(B) revolves the upper torso a little to the left, at that he seizes the fist of the enemy near the wrist with left (right) hand from below (with the palm up and the thumb outward). While continuing to turn to the left, A(B) turns the caught arm of the enemy with the palm upward, brings right (left) arm over the left (right) arm of the enemy and squeezes the upper part of the enemy's arm under his armpit.

Then A(B) presses with his right (left) forearm on the enemy's arm at the place of about two CUNs (6.6 cm, or 2.6 in) up the elbow upward from below and presses down with left (right) arm. As a result a fracture of the elbow occurs. **Photo 76 – "Squeezing with the armpit."**

Photo 76 - "Squeezing with the armpit."

Paragraph 14. KOU QUAN: Covering a fist.

This method is used when the enemy has seized you by your sleeve.

Explanations

B(A) seized A(B) by the right (left) sleeve with the left (right) hand. A(B) immediately raises his right (left) hand up and clasps the enemy's arm 1 CUN (3.33 cm, or 1.312 in) up the wrist from above, at that the thumb clasps from the left (right), four other fingers from the right (left). After squeezing the arm of the enemy A(B) immediately pulls back and at the same time seizes the left (right) hand of the enemy on its back with the left (right) hand from below, pushes forward and up, he himself turns a little to the left (right) at that. With a strong jerk of both arms the wrist of the enemy will be fractured. **Photo 77 –** **"Covering a fist."**

Photo 77 - "Covering a fist."

Paragraph 15. CHENG ZHOU DUAN WAN: Propping up an elbow and fracture a wrist.

The methods mentioned in paragraphs 15 and 16 can be successfully used only by a well-trained combatant as one should be able to take an advantageous position to execute them but it needs some experience.

This method is used when if in the course of a fight both of combatants have fallen on the ground.

Explanations

In the course of a fight B(A) falls down on the ground, A(B) must fall together with him as to be on the left of the enemy. At the same moment A(B) squeezes, between his legs, the left (right) enemy's arm with its palm up. The left (right) leg of A(B) is moved a little forward and the right (left) leg backward, thus the upper part of the left (right) arm of B(A) lies on the left (right) leg of A(B) and the lower part of the left (right) arm of B(A) is pressed by the right (left) leg of A(B) from above. A(B) raises a little the left (right) leg and presses down with the right (left) leg. At the same time A(B) seizes the right (left) hand of the enemy with his right (left) hand and pulls it to the right (left) shoulder of the enemy. Simultaneously A(B) thrusts his left (right) hand under the right (left) armpit of B(A), seizes him by the forearm near the wrist and pulls back with force. As a consequence of those actions there will be a fracture of left (right) elbow and the right (left) wrist of the enemy. **Photo 78 – "Propping up an elbow and fracturing a wrist."**

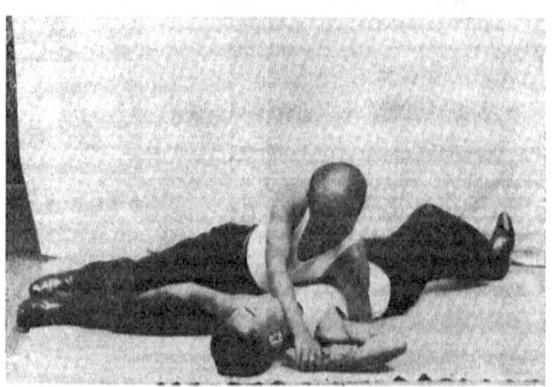

Photo 78 – "Propping up an elbow and fracturing a wrist."

Paragraph 16. BE ZHOU: Squeezing an elbow.

This method is used to fracture enemy's elbow joint when in the course of a fight he falls down or sits on the ground.

Explanations

B(A) tries to get up after falling. At that moment A(B) instantly seizes the left (right) arm of B(A) with both hands, quickly brings right (left) leg over the head of the enemy and presses back with right (left) leg. A(B) twists the left (right) arm of the enemy with both hands so that the enemy's elbow with its outer side will touch the left (right) thigh of A(B). Arms and legs of A(B) apply an effort and the elbow of the enemy will be fractured. **Photo 79 – "Squeezing an elbow."**

Photo 79 – "Squeezing an elbow."

Paragraph 17. TI ZHOU: Propping up an elbow.

It is somewhat more difficult to use this method than the method "Covering a fist" shown in photo 77.

This method is used if the enemy has seized you by the sleeve.

Explanations

B(A) seized A(B) by the right (left) sleeve with the right (left) hand. Instantly A(B) seizes from below the right (left) arm of the enemy by the wrist with his right (left) hand and strongly pulls it to himself and to the right (left), turning it with palm up. Simultaneously A(B) with the inner side of arm crook "props up" the held arm of the enemy at a point about two CUNs (6.66 cm, or 2.62 in) up the elbow. At that A(B) raises his left (right) leg bent in knee, sets the upper part of the shin against the region of the thigh joint of B(A) and pushes

Photo 80 – "Propping up an elbow."

off with force. During those actions the upper torso of A(B) turns and inclines to the right (left). In that position the left (right) arm of A(B) presses up and the right (left) arm presses down. A fracture of the elbow joint of the enemy's right (left) arm will occur. **Photo 80 – "Propping up an elbow."**

Paragraph 18. YA ZHOU: Pressing with an elbow.

If the enemy seizes your right arm with his right hand, the method XIAO CHAN SI – "Small hank of thread" (see part 6, paragraph 1) can be used. If the enemy seizes your right arm with his left hand, this method will do.

Photo 81 – "Pressing with an elbow."

Explanations

B(A) seized A(B) by the right (left) arm in the region of the wrist with his left (right) hand. A(B) instantly covers the hand of the enemy with his left (right) hand and strongly pulls with both arms toward himself, his torso turning to the left. Simultaneously A(B) presses on the caught arm of the enemy from above downward and toward himself with the right (left) elbow and inclines the upper torso forward. A fracture of the enemy's elbow will occur. **Photo 81 – "Pressing with an elbow."**

Paragraph 19. PEN AN ZHOU: Squeezing an elbow.

In this case it is necessary to take into account difference in stature.

This method is used if the enemy has seized you by your clothes in the region of the waist.

Explanations

B(A) seized A(B) by the clothes in the region of the waist on the left (right) side with his right (left) hand. Instantly A(B) quickly inclines the upper part of his torso forward, hooks the arm of the enemy a little bit up the elbow with the inner side of the left (right) arm crook and raises it up with force. Simultaneously A(B) puts his right (left) hand on the upper part of the right (left) arm of the enemy and presses down, seizes his right (left) arm a little bit up the elbow with his left (right) hand. After having seized the arm of the enemy in

Photo 82 – "Squeezing an elbow."

such a manner, A(B) straightens up his waist, at that he props up with the left (right) arm from below and presses down with the right (left) arm. Those actions will result in a fracture of the elbow joint of the enemy. **Photo 82 – "Squeezing an elbow."**

Paragraph 20. JIA ZHOU: Clutching an elbow.

To use this method, it is necessary to snatch convenient time and act fast.

This method is used if the enemy fell down.

Photo 83 – "Clutching an elbow."

Explanations

In the course of a combat B(A) fell to the ground. A(B) must instantly dash to him from above and pin the enemy to the ground with the right (left) side, the right (left) leg of A(B) being in front with the knee set against the right (left) shoulder of the enemy. A(B) with his right (left)-sided chest ribs presses himself to the chest of the enemy and does not allow him to turn over. As a rule, after finding himself in such a position B(A) starts to wave his arms helter-skelter and tries to strike or seize the enemy. A(B) uses it to seize the right (left) arm of the enemy with the left (right) hand and press its upper part to the inner side of his right (left) thigh. Then A(B) with his left (right) leg from above pins the forearm of the right (left) arm of the enemy to the ground. A fracture of the elbow joint will occur. **Photo 83 – "Clutching an elbow."**

Paragraph 21. KUA MA: Straddling a horse.

It should be taken into account that this method can be successfully employed if you take advantage of enemy's confusion, otherwise it is extremely difficult to do!

This method is used when the enemy has fallen to the ground in the course of a combat.

Explanations

In the course of a combat B(A) falls down on his left (right) side. Usually, while falling down, a man loses, if only for an instant, his concentration. Taking advantage of that circumstance, A(B) immediately seizes, with both hands, the right (left) arm of the enemy, at the same time he steps over the

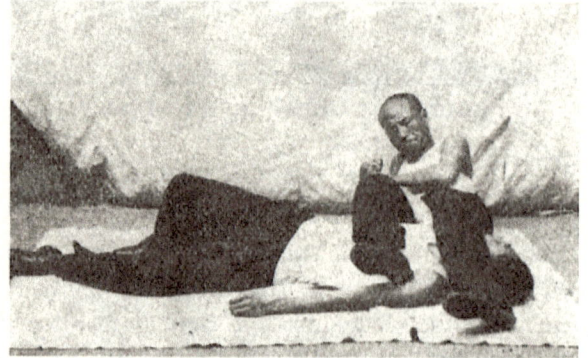

Photo 84 – "Straddling a horse."

enemy's head with left (right) leg. Then, keeping the body weight on the right (left) leg, A(B) quickly sits down on the ground near the right (left) cheek of the enemy, raises right (left) leg, puts it on the enemy's chest and presses the caught arm of the enemy with its upper part to his right (left) thigh. Arms of A(B) press down with force, his right thigh pushes up and his left leg presses the head of the enemy to the ground, at that the left (right) foot's heel sets against the ground. Due to those actions a fracture of the right (left) elbow of the enemy occurs. **Photo 84 – "Straddling a horse."**

Paragraph 22. FEN BI: Parting apart arms.

This method is used when in the course of a combat the enemy has fallen on the ground. Both arms of the enemy can be fractured by this method.

Explanations

In the course of a combat B(A) falls down. A(B) instantly straddles the enemy, pins him to the ground with the whole of his body, presses on his stomach and the chest with the aim of hampering his breathing and not allowing him to turn over. As a rule, after finding himself in such a situation B(A) tries to seize A(B) by the throat or face and throw off the enemy. A(B) uses it to seize both arms of the enemy by the wrists and part them apart, at

Photo 85 – " Parting apart arms."

the same time he presses inward with both knees which set against the upper part of enemy's arms on sides. A fracture of both elbow joints of the enemy will occur. **Photo 85 – " Parting apart arms."**

Paragraph 23. LE ZHOU: Unbending an elbow.

Here is considered a case when the enemy is lying on his side, which happens quite seldom. More often the enemy lies on his back and in that case it is better to kneel.

This method is used if in the course of a combat the enemy has fallen to the ground.

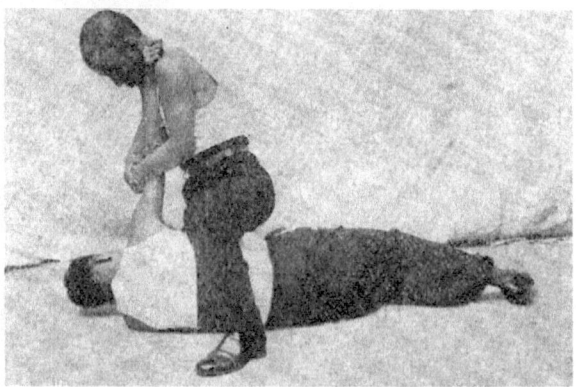

Photo 86 - "Unbending an elbow."

Explanations

B(A) falls to the ground. Seizing the opportunity, A(B) immediately straddles him. Finding himself in such a position, B(A) tries to resist with both arms. For example, B(A) tries to seize A(B) with the right (left) hand. In that case A(B) pushes the arm of the enemy with his right (left) arm to the left (right) so that the enemy's hand should be between the left (right) shoulder and the neck of A (B). Simultaneously A(B) covers the elbow of B(A) with both of his arms and presses to the right (left) and toward himself with force, propping up with left (right) shoulder forward. The effort must be fast and strong, in that case a fracture of the elbow will occur. **Photo 86: "Unbending an elbow."**

SHAOLIN CHIN NA

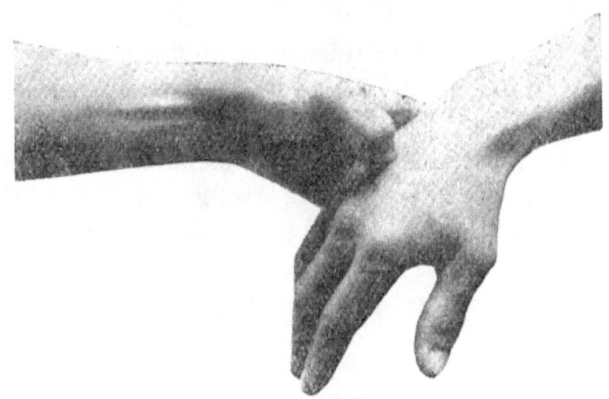

Part VII.
SHOU ZHI BU
Grips on the Hand and Fingers

Paragraph 1. TIAO MA JIN: Pressing on a tendon to cause numbing.

Below are given four methods **(photo 87 – 90)** which make it possible to free oneself from a grip of the enemy. In all four cases pressure is done by a thumb on the "tendon of numbing" on the hand of the enemy, due to it enemy's fingers unclench.

It is necessary to keep in mind points location on the hand well, additionally it is necessary to have strong, well-trained fingers to be sure of success.

Those methods are used if the enemy has seized you with his hand.

1.1 TIAO MA JIN: Use of force at the tendon to cause numbing - the first alternative.

Explanations

There are three so-called "points of numbing" on the back of the hand: **point 1** between the forefinger and middle finger, **point 2** between the middle and fourth finger and **point 3** between the fourth and little finger. All three points are located on the back of the hand, in the middle of the palm approximately, that is at an equal distance from the wrist and finger phalanxes. If you press a finger to the back of a hand in different places, you will feel projecting tendons which extend from fingers to the wrist and feel hollows between tendons. In those hollows are points you seek. If the enemy seized you, you can make the enemy unclench the hand by using force at those points. However, successful employment of this method needs exercising and strengthening fingers for a long time. Otherwise, you hardly overwhelm a serious enemy.

As a whole, the technique of pressure at all three points is the same, only places of application are different. For example, when you use force at **point 3**, you press onto the hollow between tendons of the little finger and the fourth finger of the enemy with your thumb, simultaneously you press toward the thumb from the side of the enemy's palm with your middle finger. It is necessary to press not with finger pads but with finger tips. If you do everything in the proper way, the arm of the enemy will become completely numb and numbing will spread further over his body. **Photo 87: "Use of force at the tendon to cause numbing - the first alternative."**

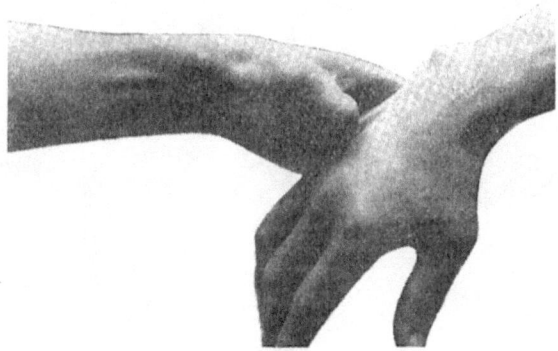

Photo 87: "Use of force at the tendon to cause numbing - the first alternative."

1.2 TIAO MA JIN: Use of force at the tendon to cause numbing - the second alternative.

Explanations

The technique of pressure at **point 2** is similar to the above, but now it is necessary to press with the thumb onto the hollow between tendons of the middle and fourth fingers and press with the middle finger toward the thumb from the side of the palm respectively. The same is use of force at point 3, so we shall not repeat the explanation. **Photo 88: "Use of force at the tendon to cause numbing - the second alternative."**

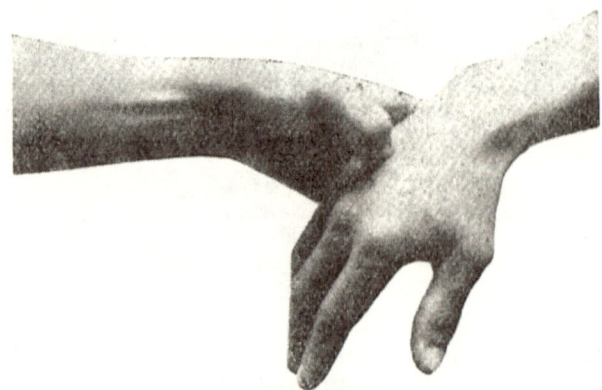

Photo 88: "Use of force at the tendon to cause numbing - the second alternative."

1.3 JIA HU KOU: Pressing on HU KOU.

Explanations

The point **HU KOU**, lit. "Tiger's jaws", lies in the space between the thumb and forefinger. If the enemy stretches out his arm with the intention of seizing you, you must immediately seize him by the wrist with one hand and press the tip of your thumb of the other hand on the point HU KOU of the enemy. It is necessary to press inward, on the tendon of his forefinger which is also a "tendon of numbing", with the tip of your thumb. Pressure must be strong to cause pain and numbing in the enemy, in that case his hand will unclench. **Photo 89: "Pressing on HU KOU."**

Photo 89: "Pressing on HU KOU."

1.4 DING QUAN: Splitting a fist.

Explanations

The enemy stretches out his arm with the intention of seizing you. You must immediately seize his arm by the wrist and press on the tendon between his middle and fourth fingers with the thumb of the other hand. It is necessary to press forward with the thumb using force and pull back toward you with the other arm. As a result of it the whole arm of the enemy will become numb. **Photo 90: "Splitting a fist."**

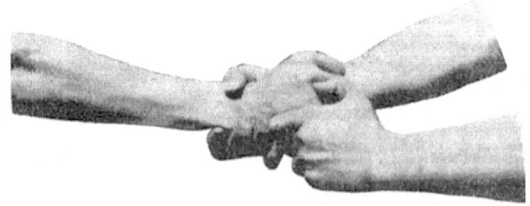

Photo 90: "Splitting a fist."

Paragraph 2. TUI ZHI: Pushing a thumb.

This method is used when the enemy attacks from the front and delivers a punch. It results in fracturing the thumb of the enemy.

Explanations

The enemy delivers a punch in the region of your chest with his right (left) fist. You must dodge to the left (right) and at the same time seize the attacking arm of the enemy by the wrist with your left (right) hand. It is necessary, within the same second, to set the right (left) palm against the thumb of the enemy from the front and push it forward and down with force and pull to yourself and upward with the left (right) arm. It will result in fracturing the thumb of the right (left) hand of the enemy. **Photo 91: "Pushing a thumb."**

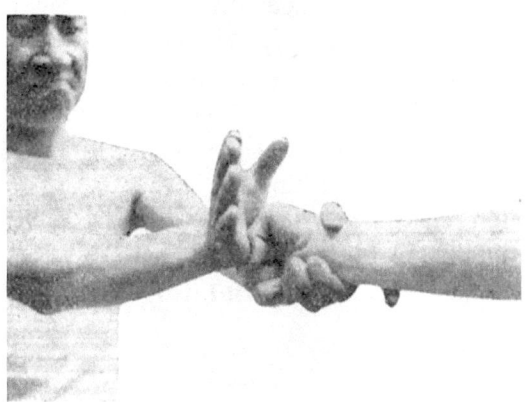

Photo 91: "Pushing a thumb."

Paragraph 3. JUAN ZHI: Bending a finger.

This method does not require great effort and high level of skill. It can be employed at any moment and in any situation. It is in strict conformity to the principle "to achieve the great with small effort".

Explanations

The enemy stretches out his arm with the intention of seizing you. You must forestall the enemy and seize him by the forefinger as to bend it. At that your thumb presses on the finger of the enemy from above and your forefinger from below, not allowing the finger of the enemy to unbend. The enemy can be seized not only by the forefinger but by the middle finger, the fourth finger or the small finger as well. After having seized the finger of the enemy in such a way, it is necessary to press on it with your thumb down and from yourself and with the forefinger up and toward yourself, three other fingers of yours close up with each other and support your forefinger to increase its actions. As a result of it the enemy will feel violent pain and his finger will be broken. If necessary, you can seize him by the wrist with the other hand to be sure that he will not free himself. To prevent the finger from being broken, it is necessary to decrease pressure a little. In this position the enemy loses his ability to resist, he can be escorted to a necessary place. **Photo 92: "Bending a finger."**

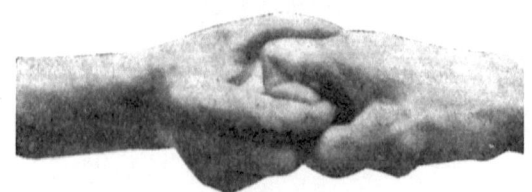

Photo 92: "Bending a finger."

Paragraph 4. QIAN YANG: Pulling the ram.

This method must be executed deftly, smoothly and at the same time fast.

This method is used when the enemy strikes you with an open palm on the face or breast or stretches out his arm with the intention of seizing you.

Photo 93: "Pulling the ram."

Explanations

B(A) strikes on the face or breast of A(B) with the right (left) palm or tries to seize him by the face or clothes. A(B) instantly seizes the forefinger or the middle finger of the attacking hand of the enemy. A(B) presses on the caught finger from himself with his thumb and toward himself and downward with the other four fingers. Simultaneously the upper part of the body of A(B) leans forward. A fracture of the finger of the enemy will occur. **Photo 93: "Pulling the ram."**

Paragraph 5. FEN ZHI: Spreading fingers.

If this method is used, a fracture of enemy's fingers will occur, he will practically lose his ability to resist. Besides, when arresting a criminal, the method can be used to escort him and force him to go in a necessary direction.

Explanations

A(B) with his left (right) hand, palm up, seizes the thumb of the left (right) hand of B(A). At the same time A(B) seizes the forth finger and small finger of the same hand of B(A) with his right (left) hand. A(B) pulls to sides and a little upward with both arms, at the same time he sets the upper part of the right (left) arm against the elbow of the held arm of the enemy and closely presses himself to the enemy with the torso. In that position the enemy can be forced to go in a necessary direction. If necessary, a fracture of fingers can be

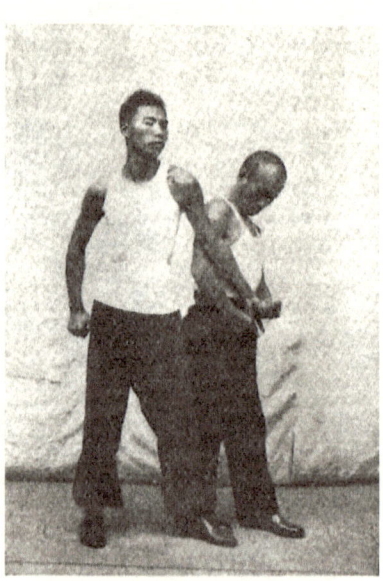

Photo 94 – "Spreading fingers."

achieved. **Photo 94: "Spreading fingers."**

SHAOLIN CHIN NA

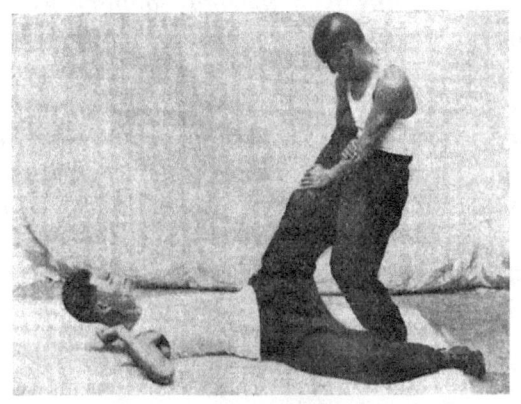

Part VIII.

YIN TUI JIAO BU
Grips on the Genitalia, Legs and Feet

Paragraph 1. ZHUA YIN: Seizing by genitalia.

Grip for genital organs is a mortally dangerous method. The position shown in the photo is somewhat simplified for the sake of convenient photographing, it bears a weak resemblance to reality of an actual combat. However, the methods given below can be used very effectively. While striking with two fingers, it is necessary to lean a little forward and crouch so that your shoulders will be on the level of the enemy's eyes or a little lower, in that case your blow will be the most destructive. At the same time your left hand must firmly seize the wrist of the enemy and pull it down and toward yourself.

Explanations

B(A) seizes A(B) by the genitalia with his right (left) hand. Instantly A(B) must seize the attacking hand of the enemy by the wrist with left (right) hand and make a pull toward himself and down, concurrently deliver a thrust to the enemy's eyes with the straightened forefinger and middle finger of the right (left) hand. At that moment the enemy involuntarily unclenches his hand. **Photo 95: "Seizing by genitalia."**

Photo 95 - "Seizing by genitalia."

When in the course of a combat the enemy seizes you by genitalia, it is extremely dangerous. You may have no time to use common methods of freeing yourself from a grip, that is affecting the "tendon of numbing", pressing on the

- 134 -

point HU KOU etc. It is necessary to act with utmost resolution and take radical measures, for example, finger thrust to eyes or other "deadly" methods. You must not be slow and hesitate for a single moment, otherwise the situation can end in lamentable result for you.

Paragraph 2. DUAN TUI: Breaking a leg.

Three methods described below are used during a combat in lying position when both opponents fell on the ground in the course of a fight. When detaining a criminal, it is necessary to take him alive, all three methods are used just for that purpose. Perhaps, from the point of view of WU SHU (the Martial Art) those methods look somewhat artificial and pretentious; as you know, the main thing in WU SHU is to disable the enemy, the simpler and faster the better. But those methods can be indispensable for capture of criminals.

If this method is used during a combat on the ground, a leg of the enemy can be broken.

Photo 96 - "Breaking a leg."

Explanations

B(A), being in a lying or sitting position, started to clasp A(B) with legs with the aim of squeezing the waist of A(B). At that moment A(B) shoves through his right (left) leg under the thigh of the left (right) leg of the enemy, raises his foot and carries it near the stomach of the enemy to the left (right), then presses with the instep and the upper part of the right (left) foot to the right (left) side of the enemy. Concurrently with those actions A(B) seizes the right (left) arm of the enemy with both arms and pulls it toward himself with force, the left (right) foot sets against the right (left) thigh of the enemy. In this position A(B) pulls the arm of the enemy toward himself with force and pushes off with his left (right) foot, the body of A(B) turning to the left (right) and leaning back. The right (left) leg of A(B) straightens with force and a fracture of the left (right) leg of B(A) occurs. **Photo 96: "Breaking a leg."**

Paragraph 3. ZUO TUI: Getting astride a leg.

If in the coarse of a combat the enemy fell on the ground, it is possible to break a leg with this method.

Explanations

In the course of a hand-to-hand combat the enemy fell on his back. Using that opportunity, A(B) swiftly puts his leg between legs of the fallen enemy, concurrently turning to him with his back, and sits down on the leg of the enemy a little up the knee. Then A(B) clasps the heel of the enemy from below with both hands and pulls up with force, simultaneously he leans with the whole of his torso back fast and shifts body weight on buttocks with which he energetically pushes the caught leg of the enemy down. It results in fracturing the leg of the enemy. **Photo 97: "Getting astride a leg."**

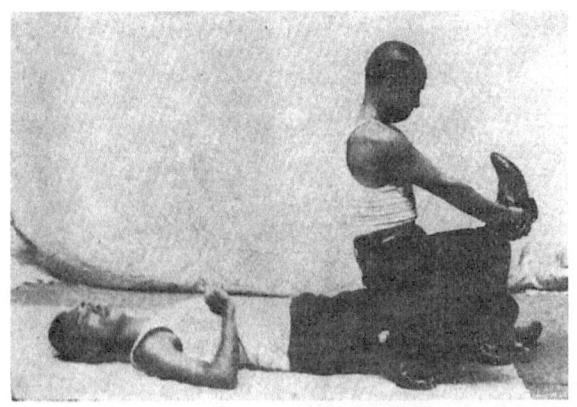

Photo 97 - "Getting astride a leg."

Paragraph 4. DENG TUI: Pushing a leg.

If in the course of a hand-to-hand combat you suddenly fell on the ground, using this method, you will be able to win in the losing position, as it seemed to be.

Explanations

In the course of a combat A(B) fell on the ground. Using this opportunity, B(A) approaches the fallen enemy and punches with the right (left) fist on his head. A(B) supporting on his right (left) arm seizes the attacking arm of the enemy by the

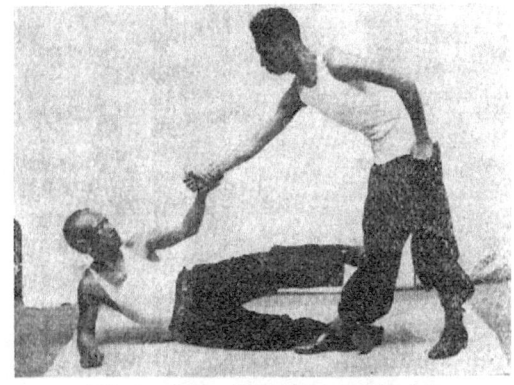

Photo 98 - "Pushing a leg."

wrist with the left (right) hand and pulls toward himself and down. Concurrently A(B) hooks the right (left) leg of the enemy a little up the heel with the instep of the right (left) foot from behind and sets his left (right) sole against the knee of the enemy. With coordinated effort of one arm and legs A(B) knocks the enemy down. If A(B) applies rather quick and strong effort, the leg of the enemy will be broken. This method can be also used without seizing arm of the enemy, only with legwork. **Photo 98: "Pushing a leg."**

Paragraph 5. DUAN ZU: Breaking an ankle.

This method is used if the enemy kicks standing or lying on the ground.

Photo 99: "Breaking an ankle."

Explanations

B(A) lying on the ground suddenly kicks with the left (right) leg. A(B) catches up the leg of the enemy with both hands from below and squeezes it under the right (left) armpit, strongly pressing to his side with the upper part of the right (left) arm. Then A(B) immediately puts the palm of the left (right) hand on the shin of the enemy, a little up the knee, shoves his right arm under the leg of the enemy and seizes the forearm of his own left (right) arm with that right hand. In that position A(B) presses on the shin-bone of the enemy from above downward with his left (right) arm as strong as possible and presses on enemy's Achilles (calcaneal) tendon from below upward with his right (left) forearm. At that A(B) leans his upper torso back and sticks out his breast forward and upward. As a consequence of those actions a fracture of the mortis joint of B(A) will occur. **Photo 99: "Breaking an ankle."**

***

Shaolin Kung Fu Online Library
www.kungfulibrary.com

Chinese Martial Arts - Theory & Practice
Old Chinese Books, Treatises, Manuscripts

Lam Sai Wing. Moving Along the Hieroglyph Gung, I Tame the Tiger with the Pugilistic Art.

Lam Sai Wing. Tiger and Crane Double Form.

Lam Sai Wing. TIET SIN: Iron Thread.

Jin Jing Zhong. Training Methods of 72 Arts of Shaolin.

Jin Jing Zhong. Dian Xue Shu: Skill of Acting on Acupoints.

Liu Jin Sheng. CHIN NA FA: Skill of Catch and Hold.

Tang Ji Ren. Pugilistic Art of the Tang Family. DA HONG QUAN.

Xu Yi Qian. CHUAN NA QUAN: Style of Piercing Blows and Holds.

Yuan Chu Cai. MEI HUA ZHUANG: Poles of Plum Blossom. External and Internal Training.

 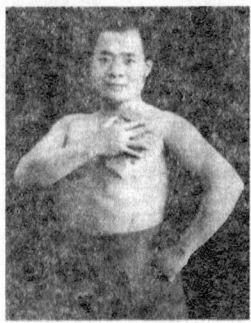 

www.ingramcontent.com/pod-product-compliance
Lightning Source LLC
Chambersburg PA
CBHW021205130626
46554CB00005B/1993